The Interesting Narrative of the Life of
Olaudah Equiano, or Gustavus Vassa, the
African. Written by Himself. Second Edition.
of 2

Olaudah Equiano

or

GUSTAVUS VASSA,

THE

INTERESTING NARRATIVE

OF

THE LIFE

OF

OLAUDAH EQUIANO,

OR

GUSTAVUS VASSA,

THE AFRICAN.

WRITTEN BY HIMSELF

VOL I.

*Behold, God is my falvation I will truft and not be
afraid, for the Lord Jehovah is my ftrength and my
fong, he alfo is become my falvation
And in that day fhall ye fay, Praife the Lord, call upon
his name, declare his doings among the people.*
Ifaiah XII. 2, 4

SECOND EDITION.

LONDON

Printed and fold for the AUTHOR, by T. WILKINS,
No. 23, Aldermanbury,

Sold alfo by Mr Johnfon, St Paul's Church-Yard,
Mr Buckland, Paternofter Row, Meffrs. Robfon
and Clark, Bond-Street, Mr Davis, oppofite
Gray's-Inn, Holborn, Mr Matthews, Strand,
Mr Stockdale, Piccadilly, Mr. Richardfon, Royal
Exchange, Mr. Kearfley, Fleet-Street, and the
Bookfellers in Oxford and Cambridge.

[Entered at Stationers-hall.]

1789.

To the Lords Spiritual and Temporal, and the Commons of the Parliament of Gieat Britain.

My Lords and Gentlemen,

PERMIT me, with the greateſt deference and reſpect, to lay at your feet the following genuine Narrative; the chief deſign of which is to excite in your auguſt aſſemblies a ſenſe of compaſſion for the miſeries which the Slave-Trade has entailed on my unfortunate countrymen. By the horrors of that trade was I firſt torn away from all the tender connexions that were naturally dear to my heart; but theſe,

through

through the myfterious wa s of
Providence, I ought to regard as
infinitely more than compenfated
by the introduction I have thence
obtained to the knowledge of the
Chriftian religion, and of a nation
which, by its liberal fentiments,
its humanity, the glorious freedom
of its government, and its proficiency
in arts and fciences, has exalted
the dignity of human nature.

I am fenfible I ought to entreat
your pardon for addreffing to you
a work fo wholly devoid of literary
merit; but, as the production of
an unlettered African, who is actuated
by the hope of becoming an
inftrument towards the relief of
his fuffering countrymen, I truft
that *fuch a man*, pleading in *fuch a*

2   *caufe,*

cause, will be acquitted of boldness and presumption.

May the God of heaven inspire your hearts with peculiar benevolence on that important day when the question of Abolition is to be discussed, when thousands, in consequence of your Determination, are to look for Happiness or Misery!

I am,

MY LORDS AND GENTLEMEN,

Your most obedient,

And devoted humble Servant,

OLAUDAH EQUIANO,

O R

GUSTAVUS VASSA.

No. 10, Union-Street, Mary-le-bone,
Dec. 24, 1789.

A
LIST
OF
SUBSCRIBERS.

His Royal Highnefs the Prince of Wales.
His Royal Highnefs the Duke of York.
His Royal Highnefs the Duke of Cumberland.

A

The Right Hon. the Earl of Ailefbury
Admiral Affleck
Mr. William Abington, 2 copies
Mr. John Abraham
James Adair, Efq.

Reverer.

SUBSCRIBERS.

The Reverend Charles Adams
Miss Mary Adams
John Ady
The Reverend Mr. Aldridge
Mr John Almon
Mrs. Arnot
Mr. Joseph Armitage
Mr. Joseph Ashpinshaw
Mrs. Ashman
Mr. Samuel Atkins
Mr John Attwood
Mr. Thomas Attwood
Mr. Ashwell
J. C. Ashworth, Esq.
Mr. Audley
Mr Aufrere

B

His Grace the Duke of Bedford
Her Grace the Duchess of Buccleugh
The Right Reverend the Lord Bishop of Bangor
The Right Hon. Lord Belgrave
The Reverend Doctor Baker
Mrs. Baker
Matthew Baillie, M D.
Mrs. Baillie
Miss Baillie
Miss J. Baillie
David Barclay, Esq.
Mr. Robert Barrett
Mr. William Barrett
Mr. John Barnes
Mr. John Basnett
Mr. Bateman

Mr.

SUBSCRIBERS.

Mrs. Baynes, 2 copies
Mr. Thomas Bellamy
Admiral George Belfour
Mr. J. Benjafield
Mr, William Bennett
Mr. Bensley
Mr. Samuel Benson
Mrs. Benton
The Reverend Mr. Bently
Mr Thomas Bentley
Mr J. P Berthon
Sir John Berney, Bart.
Alexander Blair, Esq.
James Bocock, Esq.
Mrs. Bond
Miss Bond
Mrs. Borckhardt
Mrs. E. Boverie
Alderman Boydell
Mr Harris Bottisham
————Brand, Esq.
Mr. Martin Brander
F. J. Brown, Esq. M. P. 2 copies
W Buttall, Esq.
Mr. Buxton
Mr. R. L. B.
Mr. Thomas Burton, 6 copies
Mr. W. Button
Mr Barton
Edward Burch, Esq. R. A.
Mr Marcus Butcher

C

The Right Hon. Lord Cathcart
The Right Reverend Lord Bishop of Chester

SUBSCRIBERS

The Right Hon. H. S Conway
Lady Almiria Carpenter
Charles Carter, Efq.
Mr. James Chalmers
Mr. Child
Captain John Clarkfon, of the Royal Navy
The Rev. Mr. Thomas Clarkfon, 2 copies
Mr. R. Clav
Mr. William Clout
Mr George Club
Mr. John Cobb
Mifs Calwell
Mr. Thomas Cooper
Mr. Thomas Cooper, Jun.
Richard Cofway, Efq.
Mr. James Coxe
Mr. J. C.
Mr. Croucher
Mr. Cruickfhanks
Ottobah Cugoano, or John Stewart
Mr. Jofeph Chamberlain

D

The Right Hon. the Earl of Dartmouth
The Right Hon. the Earl of Derby
Sir William Dolben, Bart.
Mr. John Dalby
Mrs. M. Davey
Mr. Davis
The Reverend C. E. De Coetlogon
John Delamain, Efq.
Mrs. Delamain,

Mr.

SUBSCRIBERS.

Mr. William Denton
Mr. T. Dickie
Mr. William Dickfon
Mr. Charles Dilly, 2 copies
Andrew Drummond, Efq.
Mr. George Durant
Mr E. O. Donovan
The Reverend Mr. William Dunn

E

The Right Hon. the Earl of Effex
The Right Hon. the Countefs of Effex
Sir Gilbert Elliot, Bart. 2 copies
Lady Ann Erfkine
G. Noel Edwards, Efq M. P. 2 copies
Mr. Durs Egg
Mr Ebenezer Evans
The Reverend Mr. John Eyre
Mr. William Eyre
Mr. John Elgar

F

Mr. George Fallowdown
Mr. John Fell
Mrs. William Fielding
F W. Fofter, Efq.
The Reverend Mr. Fofter
Mr. J. Frith
W. Fuller, Efq.

The

SUBSCRIBERS.

G

The Right Hon. the Earl of Gainsborough
The Right Hon. the Earl of Grosvenor
The Right Hon. Viscount Gallway
The Right Hon. Viscountess Gallway
————Gardener, Esq.
Mrs Garrick
Mr John Gates
Mr Samuel Gear
Mr Richard George
Sir Philip Gibbes, Bart. 6 copies
Miss Gibbes
Mr. Edward Gilbert
Mr Jonathan Gillett
W. P. Gillies, Esq.
Mrs. Gordon
Mr. Grange
Mr. William Grant
Mr. John Grant
Mr. Adam Graham
Mr. R. Greening
S. Griffiths
John Grove, Esq.
Mrs. Guerin
The Reverend Mr. Gwinnup

H

The Right Hon. the Earl of Hopetoun
The Right Hon. Lord Hawke
The Right Hon. Countess Harrington
Right Hon. Dowager Countess of Huntingdon

Mr.

SUBSCRIBERS.

Mr. Benjamin Haigh
Charles Hamilton, Efq.
Thomas Hall, Efq.
Mr. Hall
Mr. Haley
Thomas Hammerfley, Efq.
Mr. Timothy Hansfield
Hugh Jofiah Hanfard, Efq.
Mrs Harben
Mr. Mofes Hart
Mr. Thomas Hardy
Mr. Hafzelegrove
Mrs. Hawkins
Mr. Hayfom
Mr. Hearne
Mr William Hepburn
Mr. J. Hibbert
Mr. Jacob Higman
Sir Richard Hill, Bart.
Reverend Mr. Rowland Hill
Mifs Hill
Captain John Hills, Royal Navy
Edmund Hill, Efq.
The Reverend Mr. Edward Hoare
William Hodges, Efq.
Mrs. Hogflefh
The Reverend Mr. John Holmes, 3 copies
Mr. Martin Hopkins
Mr. Thomas Howell
Mr. R. Huntley
Mr. J. Hunt
Mr. Philip Hurlock, Sen.
Mr. Hutfon
Mr. Hodgkinfon
Mr. Abraham Horsfall
Mr. John Horsfall
Mr. Robert Hudfon
Mr. George Hutton

SUBSCRIBERS.

J

Mr. T. W. J. Efq.
Mr. James Jackfon
Mr. Thomas Jackfon
Mr. John Jackfon
Mr James Jacobs
Reverend Mr. James
Mr. Jefferys, Royal Navy
Mrs. Anne Jennings
The Reverend Dr. Jowett
Mr Johnfon
Mrs. Johnfon
Mr. William Jones
Mr. James Jones
Thomas Irving, Efq. 3 copies
Mr. William Juftins
Edward Ind, Efq.
Robert Ind, Efq.
James Johnfon, Efq.

K

The Right Hon. Lord Kinnaird
William Kendal, Efq.
James Karr, Efq.
Mr. William Ketland
Mr. Edward King
Mr. Thomas Kingfton
The Reverend Dr. Kippis
Mr. William Kitchener
Mr. John Knight

The

L

The Right Reverend the Lord Bishop of London
Mr John Laifne
Mr John Lamb
Bennet Langton, Efq.
Mr S. Lee
Mr. Walter Lewis
Mr. Walter Lewis, Jun.
Mr. J. Lewis
Mr. J. Lindfey
Mr. T. Litchfield
Edward Loveden Loveden, Efq. M. P.
Charles Lloyd, Efq.
Mr. William Lloyd
Mr. Samuel Lucas
Mr. J. B. Lucas
Mr. James Luken
Henry Lyte, Efq.
Mrs. Lyon

M

His Grace the Duke of Marlborough
His Grace the Duke of Montague
The Right Hon. Lord Mulgrave
Sir Herbert Mackworth, Bart.
Sir Charles Middleton, Bart.
Lady Middleton
Mr. Thomas Macklane
Mr. George Markett

James

SUBSCRIBERS.

James Martin, Efq. M. P
Mafter Martin, Hayes-Grove, Kent
Mr. William Maffey
Mr. Jofeph Maffingham
Mr. Matthews, 6 copies
John M'Intofh, Efq
Paul Le Mefurier, Efq. M. P. 3 copies
Mr James Mewburn
The Reverend H Michel
Mr. N. Middleton
T. Mitchell, Efq.
Mrs. Montague, 2 copies
Mifs Hannah More
Mr. George Morrifon
Thomas Morris, Efq,
Mifs Morris
Morris Morgann, Efq
Mr Mufgrove
Mr Thomas Mufgrove
Mr. P. M.

N

His Grace the Duke of Northumberland
Henry Naylor, Efq.
Francis Noble, Efq.
Captain Norman, Royal Navy
Captain Nurfe

O

Edward Ogle, Efq.
James Ogle, Efq.

Robert

SUBSCRIBERS.

Robert Oliver, Efq.
The Reverend Mr J. Owen

P

The Right Hon. William Pickett, Efq.
    Lord Mayor of London
Mr. D. Parker
Mr. W. Parker
Mr O Parry
Mr. Richard Packer, Jun.
The Reverend Dr Peckard of Cambridge
Mr James Pearfe
Mr. J. Pearfon
J. Penn, Efq.
George Peters, Efq.
Mr. W. Phillips
J. Phillips, Efq.
Mrs. Pickard
Mr. Charles Pilgrim
The Hon. George Pitt, M. P.
Mr. Thomas Pooley
Patrick Power, Efq.
Mr. Michael Power
Jofeph Pratt, Efq.
Mr. Samuel Purle
Mr. M. P.

Q

His Grace the Duke of Queenfberry
Robert Quarme, Efq.

The

R

The Right Hon. Lord Rawdon
The Right Hon. Lord Rivers, 2 copies
Lieutenant General Rainsford
Reverend James Ramsay, 3 copies
Mr. S. Remnant, Jun.
Mr. William Richards, 2 copies
Mr. J. C. Robarts
Mr. James Roberts
Dr. Robinson
Mr. Robinson
Mr. C Robinson
Admiral Roddam
George Rose, Esq. M. P.
Mr. W. Ross
Mr. William Rouse
Mr. Walter Row

S

His Grace the Duke of St. Albans
Her Grace the Duchess of St. Albans
The Right Reverend the Lord Bishop of St. David's
The Right Hon Earl Stanhope, 3 copies
The Right Hon the Earl of Scarbrough
Mr Sampson
William, the Son of Ignatius Sancho
Mrs. Mary Ann Sandiford
Mr. William Sawyer
Mr. Thomas Seddon
W. Seward, Esq,

Granville

SUBSCRIBERS.

Reverend Mr. Thomas Scott
Granville Sharp, Efq 2 copies
Mr. Richard Shepheid
Mr. William Shill
Captain Sidney Smith, of the Royal Navy
Colonel Simcoe
Mr John Simco
General Smith
John Smith, Efq.
Mr George Smith
Mr. William Smith
John James Smith
Reverend Mr Southgate
Thomas Spalding
John Spratt
Mr Charles Starkey
Thomas Steel, Efq M. P.
Mr. Staples Steare
Mr. Jofeph Stewardfon
Mr. Henry Stone, Jun. 2 copies
Mr John Strickland
John Symmons, Efq,
Mr. William Symonds

T

Dr. Thackeray
Henry Thornton, Efq. M. P.
The Reverend Robeit Thornton
Mr Abraham Thorp
Alexander Thomfon, M. D.
The Reverend Mr. John Till
Mr. Samuel Townly
Mr. Daniel Trinder

The

SUBSCRIBERS.

The Reverend Mr. C. La Trobe
Clement Tudway, Efq.
Mrs. Twifden

U

Mr. M. Underwood

V

Mr. John Vaughan
Mrs. Vendt

W

The Right Hon. Earl of Warwick
The Right Reverend the Lord Bishop of Worcefter
The Hon. William Windham, Efq. M. P.
Mr. C. B. Wadftrom
Mr. George Walne
The Reverend Mr. Ward
Mr. S. Warren
Mr. J. Waugh
Jofiah Wedgwood, Efq.
The Reverend Mr. John Wefley
Mr J. Wheble
Samuel Whitbread, Efq M P.
The Reverend Mr Thomas Wigzell
Mr W. Wilfon
The Reverend Mr Wills
Mr Thomas Wimfett
Mr William Winchefter
The Reverend Elhanan Winchefter, 6 copies

The

J.   , Efq.
Mr   ood
Mr. Joseph Woods
Mr John Wood
J Wright, Efq
Mr William Watfon
Mr James Welch
Mrs Willmott
Mr. George Wille

Y

Mr. Yeo
Mr Samuel Yockney
Mr. Thomos Young

ERRATA.

CONTENTS

OF

VOLUME I.

CHAP.

CONTENTS.

CHAP. IV.

CHAP. V.

CHAP. VI.

THE LIFE, &c.

CHAPTER I.

The author's account of his country, and their manners and customs—Administration of justice—E. ibrenché—Marriage ceremony, and public entertainments—Mode of living—Dress—Manufactures Buildings—Commerce—Agriculture—War and religion—Superstition of the natives—Funeral ceremonies of the priests or magicians—Curious mode of discovering poison—Some hints concerning the origin of the author's countrymen, with the opinions of different writers on that subject.

I BELIEVE it is difficult for those who publish their own memoirs to escape the imputation of vanity; nor is this the only difadvantage under which they labour· it is alfo their misfortune, that what is uncommon is rarely, if ever, believed, and what is obvious we are apt to turn from with difguft, and to charge the writer with impertinence. People generally think thofe memoirs only worthy to be read or remembered which abound in great or ftriking events; thofe, in fhort, which in a high degree excite either admiration or pity: all others they confign to contempt and oblivion. It is therefore, I confefs, not a little hazardous in a private and obfcure individual, and a ftranger too, thus to folicit the indulgent attention of the public; efpecially when I own I offer here the hiftory of neither a faint, a hero, nor a tyrant. I believe there are a few events in my life, which have not happened to many: it is true the incidents of it are numerous; and, did I confider myfelf an European,

I might

I might fay my fufferings were great:
but when I compare my lot with that
of moft of my countrymen, I regard
myfelf as a *particular favourite of Heaven*, and acknowledge the meieies of
Providence in every occurrence of my
life. If then the following narrative
does not appear fufficiently interefting
to engage general attention, let my
motive be fome excufe for its publica-
tion. I am not fo foolifhly vain as to
expect from it either immortality or
literary reputation. If it affords any
fatisfaction to my numerous friends, at
whofe requeft it has been written, or
in the fmalleft degree promotes the
interefts of humanity, the ends for
which it was undertaken will be fully
attained, and every wifh of my heart
gratified. Let it therefore be remembered, that, in wifhing to avoid cenfure,
I do not afpire to praife.

That

That part of Africa, known by the name of 'Guinea, to which the trade for slaves is carried on, extends along the coast above 3400 miles, from Senegal to Angola, and includes a variety of kingdoms. Of these the most considerable is the kingdom of Benin, both as to extent and wealth, the richness and cultivation of the soil, the power of its king, and the number and various disposition of the inhabitants. It is situated nearly under the line, and extends along the coast about 170 miles, but runs back into the intertior part of Africa to a distance hitherto I believe unexplored by any traveller, and seems only terminated at length by the empire of Abyssinia, near 1500 miles from its beginning. This kingdom is divided into many provinces or districts. in one of the most remote and fertile of which,

I

I was born, in the year 1745, situated in a charming fruitful vale, named Essaka. The distance of this province from the capital of Benin and the sea coast must be very considerable; for I had never heard of white men or Europeans, nor of the sea; and our subjection to the king of Benin was little more than nominal; for every transaction of the government, as far as my slender observation extended, was conducted by the chiefs or elders of the place. The manners and government of a people who have little commerce with other countries are generally very simple, and the history of what passes in one family or village, may serve as a specimen of the whole nation. My father was one of those elders or chiefs I have spoken of, and was styled Embrenché, a term, as I remember, importing the highest distinction, and

B 3   signifying

signifying in our language a *mark* of grandeur. This mark is conferred on the person entitled to it, by cutting the skin across at the top of the forehead, and drawing it down to the eye-brows, and while it is in this situation apply-ing a warm hand, and rubbing it until it shrinks up into a thick *weal* across the lower part of the forehead. Most of the judges and senators were thus marked; my father had long borne it: I had seen it conferred on one of my brothers, and I also was *destined* to receive it by my parents. Those Em-brenché or chief men, decided disputes and punished crimes; for which pur-pose they always assembled together. The proceedings were generally short; and in most cases the law of retaliation prevailed. I remember a man was brought before my father, and the other judges, for kidnapping a boy; and,

and, although he was the son of a chief
or senator, he was condemned to make
recompenfe by a man or woman flave.
Adultery, however, was fometimes punifhed with flavery or death; a punifh-
ment which I believe is inflicted on
it throughout moft of the nations of
Africa * : fo facred among them is the
honour of the marriage bed, and fo
jealous are they of the fidelity of their
wives. Of this I recollect an inftance
—a woman was convicted before the
judges of adultery, and delivered over,
as the cuftom was, to her hufband to
be punifhed. Accordingly he determined to put her to death : but it being
found, juft before her execution, that
fhe had an infant at her breaft , and no
woman being prevailed on to perform
the part of a nurfe, fhe was fpared on

* See Benezet's " Account of Guinea"
throughout.

B 4   account

account of the child. The men, however, do not preserve the same constancy to their wives, which they expect from them, for they indulge in
a plurality, though seldom in more
than two. Their mode of marriage
is thus.—Both parties are usually betrothed when young by their parents,
(though I have known the males to
betroth themselves) On this occasion
a feast is prepared, and the bride and
bridegroom stand up in the midst of
all their friends, who are assembled for
the purpose, while he declares she is
thenceforth to be looked upon as his
wife, and that no other person is to
pay any addresses to her. This is also
immediately proclaimed in the vicinity, on which the bride retire from
the affair. Some time after she is
brought home to her husband, and
then another feast is made, to which
the

the relations of both parties are in-
vited: her parents then deliver her to
the bridegroom, accompanied with a
number of bleffings, and at the fame
time they tie round her waift a cotton
ftrmg of the thicknefs of a goofe-quill,
which none but married women are
permitted to wear fhe is now confidered as completely his wife; and at
this time the dowry is given to the
new married pair, which generally
confifts of portions of land, flaves, and
cattle, houfhold goods, and implements of hufbandry Thefe are offered by the friends of both parties;
befides which the parents of the bridegroom prefent gifts to thofe of the
bride, whofe property fhe is looked
upon before marriage, but after it fhe
is efteemed the fole property of her
hufband The ceremony being now
ended the feftival begins, which is

B 5   celebrated

celebrated with bonefires, and loud acclamations of joy, accompanied with mufic and dancing.

We are almoft a nation of dancers, muficians, and poets. Thus every great event, fuch as a triumphant return from battle, or other caufe of public rejoicing is celebrated in public dances which are accompanied with fongs and mufic fuited to the occafion. The affembly is feperated into four divifions, which dance either apart or in fuc_ ceffion, and each with a character peculiar to itfelf. The firft divifion contains the married men, who in their dances frequently exhibit feats of arms, and the repiefentation of a battle. To thefe fucceed the married women, who dance in the fecond divifion. The young men accupy the third. and the maidens the fourth. Each reprefents fome interefting fcene

of

of real life, such as a great achievement, domeftic employment, a pathetic ftory, or fome rural fport, and as the fubject is generally founded on fome recent event, it is therefore ever new. This gives our dances a fpirit and variety which I have fcarcely feen elfewhere*. We have many mufical inftruments, particularly drums of different kinds, a piece of mufic which refembles a guitar, and another much like a ftickado. Thefe laft are chiefly ufed by betrothed virgins, who play on them on all grand feftivals.

As our manners are fimple, our luxuries are few. The drefs of both fexes is nearly the fame. It generally confifts of a long piece of calico, or muflin, wrapped loofely round the body, fomewhat in the form of a

* When I was in Smyrna I have frequently feen the Greeks dance after this manner

highland

highland plaid. This is usually dyed blue, which is our favorite colour. It is extracted from a berry, and is brighter and richer than any I have seen in Europe. Besides this, our women of distinction wear golden ornaments, which they dispose with some profusion on their arms and legs. When our women are not employed with the men in tillage, their usual occupation is spinning and weaving cotton, which they afterwards dye, and make into garments. They also manufacture earthen vessels, of which we have many kinds. Among the rest tobacco pipes, made after the same fashion, and used in the same manner, as those in Turkey*.

Our manner of living is entirely plain, for as yet the natives are unac-

* The bowl is earthen, curiously figured, to which a long reed is fixed as a tube. This tube is sometimes so long as to be borne by one, and frequently out of grandeur, by two boys.

quainted

quainted with thofe refinements in cookery which debauch the tafte · bullocks, goats, and poultry, fupply the greateft part of their food. Thefe conftitute likewife the principal wealth of the country, and the chief articles of its commerce. The flefh is ufually ftewed in a pan; to make it favoury we fometimes ufe alfo pepper, and other fpices, and we have falt made of wood afhes Our vegetables are moftly plantains, eadas, yams, beans, and Indian corn. The head of the family ufually eats alone; his wives and flaves have alfo their feparate tables. Before we tafte food we always wafh our hands: indeed our cleanlinefs on all occafions is extreme, but on this it is an indifpenfible ceremony. After wafhing, libation is made, by pouring out a fmall portion of the drink on the floor, and toffing a fmall quantity of the food

in

in a certain place, for the spirits of departed relations, which the natives suppose to preside over their conduct, and guard them from evil. They are totally unacquainted with strong or spirituous liquors; and their principal beverage is palm wine. This is got from a tree of that name, by tapping it at the top, and fastening a large gourd to it, and sometimes one tree will yield three or four gallons in a night. When just drawn it is of a most delicious sweetness; but in a few days it acquires a tartish and more spirituous flavour: though I never saw any one intoxicated by it. The same tree also produces nuts and oil. Our principal luxury is in perfumes; one sort of these is an odoriferous wood of delicious fragrance. the other a kind of earth; a small portion of which thrown

2   into

into the fire diffuses a moſt powerful odour *. We beat this wood into powder, and mix it with palm oil; with which both men and women perfume themſelves.

In our buildings we ſtudy convenience rather than ornament. Each maſter of a family has a large ſquare piece of ground, ſurrounded with a moat or fence, or encloſed with a wall made of red earth tempered: which, when dry, is as hard as brick. Within this are his houſes to accommodate his family and ſlaves; which, if numerous, fiequently preſent the appearance of a village. In the middle ſtands the principal building, appropriated to the ſole uſe of the maſter, and conſiſting

---

* When I was in Smyrna I ſaw the ſame kind of earth, and brought ſome of it with me to England; it reſembles muſk in ſtrength, but is more delicious in ſcent, and is not unlike the ſmell of a roſe.

of

of two apartments, in one of which he fits in the day with his family, the other is left apart for the reception of his friends. He has befides thefe a diſtinct apartment in which he ſleeps, together with his male children. On each ſide are the apartments of his wives, who have alſo their ſeparate day and night houſes. The habitations of the ſlaves and their families are diſtributed throughout the reſt of the encloſure. Theſe houſes never exceed one ſtory in height. they are always built of wood, or ſtakes driven into the ground, croſſed with wattles, and neatly plaſtered within and without. The roof is thatched with reeds Our day-houſes are left open at the ſides, but thoſe in which we ſleep are always covered, and plaſtered in the inſide, with a compoſition mixed with cow-dung, to keep off the different inſects, which

which annoy us during the night.
The walls and floors also of these are
generally covered with mats. Our
beds consist of a platform, raised three
or four feet from the ground, on which
are laid skins, and different parts of a
spungy tree called plantain. Our
covering is calico or muslin, the same
as our dress. The usual seats are a few
logs of wood; but we have benches,
which are generally perfumed, to accommodate strangers: these compose the
greater part of our household furniture.
Houses so constructed and furnished
require but little skill to erect them.
Every man is a sufficient architect for
the purpose. The whole neighbourhood
afford their unanimous assistance in
building them, and in return receive,
and expect no other recompense than
a feast.

As we live in a country where nature

is prodigal of her favours, our wants are few and eafily fupplied, of courfe we have few manufactures. They confift for the moft part of calicoes, earthen ware, ornaments, and inftruments of war and hufbandry. But thefe make no part of our commerce, the principal articles of which, as I have obferved, are provifions. In fuch a ftate, money is of little ufe; however we have fome fmall pieces of coin, if I may call them fuch. They are made fomething like an anchor; but I do not remember either their value or denomination. We have alfo markets, at which I have been frequently with my mother. Thefe are fometimes vifited by ftout mahogany-coloured men from the fouth weft of us · we call them *Oye-Eboe*, which term fignifies red men living at a diftance. They generally bring us fire-arms, gunpowder, hats,

hats, beads, and dried fish. The last we esteemed a great rarity, as our waters were only brooks and springs. These articles they barter with us for odoriferous woods and earth, and our salt of wood ashes. They always carry flaves through our land; but the strictest account is exacted of their manner of procuring them before they are suffered to pass. Sometimes indeed we sold slaves to them, but they were only prisoners of war, or such among us as had been convicted of kidnapping, or adultery, and some other crimes, which we esteemed heinous. This practice of kidnapping induces me to think, that, notwithstanding all our strictness, their principal business among us was to trepan our people. I remember too they carried great sacks along with them, which not long after I had an.

opportunity

opportunity of fatally being applied to that infamous purpofe.

Our land is uncommonly rich and fruitful, and produces all kinds of vegetables in great abundance. We have plenty of Indian corn, and vaft quantities of cotton and tobacco. Our pine apples grow without culture; they are about the fize of the largeft fugar-loaf, and finely flavoured. We have alfo fpices of different kinds, particularly pepper; and a variety of delicious fruits which I have never feen in Europe; together with gums of various kinds, and honey in abundance. All our induftry is excited to improve thofe bleffings of nature. Agriculture is our chief employment, and every one, even the children and women, are engaged in it. Thus we are all habituated to labour from our earlieft years. Every one contributes fomething to the com-

mon

mon ftock; and as we are unacquainted with idlenefs, we have no beggars. The benefits of fuch a mode of living are obvious. The Weft India planters prefer the flaves of Benin or Eboe, to thofe of any other part of Guinea, for their hardinefs, intelligence, integrity, and zeal. Thofe benefits are felt by us in the general healthinefs of the people, and in their vigour and activity, I might have added too in their comelinefs. Deformity is indeed unknown amongft us, I mean that of fhape. Numbers of the natives of Eboe now in London, might be brought in fupport of this affertion for, in regard to complexion, ideas of beauty are wholly relative. I remember while in Africa to have feen three negro children, who were tawny, and another quite white, who were univerfally regarded by myfelf, and the natives in

2   eneral,

general, as far as related to their complexions, as deformed. Our women too were in my eyes at leaſt uncommonly graceful, alert, and modeſt to a degree of baſhfulneſs; nor do I remember to have ever heard of an inſtance of incontinence amongſt them before marriage. They are alſo remarkably cheerful. Indeed cheerfulneſs and affability are two of the leading characteriſtics of our nation.

Our tillage is exerciſed in a large plain or common, ſome hours walk from our dwellings, and all the neighbours reſort thither in a body. They uſe no beaſts of huſbandry; and their only inſtruments are hoes, axes, ſhovels, and beaks, or pointed iron to dig with. Sometimes we are viſited by locuſts, which come in large clouds, ſo as to darken the air, and deſtroy our harveſt. This however happens rarely, but when

it

it does, a famine is produced by it.
I remember an inftance or two wherein this happened. This common is
often the theatre of war; and therefore
when our people go out to till their
land, they not only go in a body,
but generally take their arms with
them for fear of a furprife; and when
they apprehend an invafion, they guard
the avenues to their dwellings, by
driving fticks into the ground, which
are fo fharp at one end as to pierce the
foot, and are generally dipt in po fon.
From what I can recollect of thefe
battles, they appear to have been irrup-
tions of one little ftate or diftrict on the
other, to obtain prifoners or booty.
Perhaps they were incited to this by
thofe traders who brought the European goods I mentioned amongft us.
Such a mode of obtaining flaves in
Africa is common; and I believe more

are

are procured this way, and by kidnaping, than any other *. When a trader wants flaves, he applies to a chief for them, and tempts him with his wares. It is not extraordinary, if on this occafion he yields to the temptation with as little firmnefs, and accepts the price of his fellow creatures liberty with as little reluctance as the enlightened merchant. Accordingly he falls on his neighbours, and a defperate battle enfues. If he prevails and takes prifoners, he gratifies his avarice by felling them; but, if his party be vanquifhed, and he falls into the hands of the enemy, he is put to death: for, as he has been known to foment their quarrels, it is thought dangerous to let him furvive, and no ranfom can fave him, though all other prifoners may be redeemed. We have firearms, bows and arrows, broad two-

* See Benezet's Account of Africa throughout.

edged

edged fwords and javelins: we have
fhields alfo which cover a man from
head to foot. All are taught the ufe
of thefe weapons; even our women are
warriors, and march boldly out to fight
along with the men. Our whole diftrict is a kind of militia: on a certain
fignal given, fuch as the firing of a gun
at night, they all rife in arms and rufh
upon their enemy. It is perhaps fomething remarkable, that when our people
march to the field a red flag or banner
is borne before them. I was once a
witnefs to a battle in our common.
We had been all at work in it one day
as ufual, when our people were fud-
denly attacked. I climbed a tree at
fome diftance, from which I beheld
the fight. There were many women as well as men on both fides;
among others my mother was there,
and armed with a broad fword. After

fighting for a confiderable time with great fury, and many had been killed, our people obtained the victory, and took their enemy's Chief prifoner. He was carried off in great triumph, and, though he offered a large ranfom for his life, he was put to death. A virgin of note among our enemies had been flain in the battle, and her arm was expofed in our market-place, where our trophies were always exhibited. The fpoils were divided according to the merit of the warriors. Thofe prifoners which were not fold or redeemed we kept as flaves. but how different was their condition from that of the flaves in the Weft Indies! With us they do no more work than other members of the community, even their mafter; their food, clothing and lodging were nearly the fame as theirs, (except that they were not permitted

to

to eat with thofe who were free-born); and theie was fcarce any other difference between them, than a fuperior degree of importance which the head of a family poffeffes in our ftate, and that authority which, as fuch, he exercifes over every part of his houfehold. Some of thefe flaves have even flaves under them as their own property, and for their own ufe.

As to religion, the natives believe that there is one Creator of all things, and that he lives in the fun, and is gurted round with a belt that he may never eat or drink; but, according to fome, he fmokes a pipe, which is our own favourite luxury. They believe he governs events, efpecially our deaths or captivity; but, as for the doctrine of eternity, I do not remember to have ever heard of it: fome however beleve in the tranfmigration of fouls in

C 2

a certain

a certain degree. Those spirits, which
are not transmigrated, such as their
dear friends or relations, they believe always attend them, and guard them from
the bad spirits or their foes. For this
reason they always before eating, as I
have observed, put some small portion
of the meat, and pour some of their
drink, on the ground for them; and
they often make oblations of the blood
of beasts or fowls at their graves. I
was very fond of my mother, and almost constantly with her. When she
went to make these oblations at her
mother's tomb, which was a kind of
small solitary thatched house, I sometimes attended her. There she made her
libations, and spent most of the night
in cries and lamentations. I have been
often extremely terrified on these occasions. The loneliness of the place,
the darkness of the night, and the ceremony

mony of libation, naturally awful and gloomy, were heightened by my mother's lamentations; and these concurring with the doleful cries of birds, by which these places were frequented, gave an inexpressible terror to the scene.

We compute the year from the day on which the sun crosses the line, and on its setting that evening, there is a general shout throughout the land; at least I can speak from my own knowledge, throughout our vicinity. The people at the same time make a great noise with rattles, not unlike the basket rattles used by children here, though much larger, and hold up their hands to heaven for a blessing. It is then the greatest offerings are made; and those children whom our wise men foretel will be fortunate are then presented to different people. I remember

many

many ufed to come to fee me, and I
was carried about to others for that
purpofe. They have many offerings,
particularly at full moons; generally
two at harveft before the fruits are
taken out of the ground: and when
any young animals are killed, fometimes they offer up part of them as a
facrifice. Thefe offerings, when made
by one of the heads of a family, ferve
for the whole. I remember we often
had them at my father's and my uncle's,
and their families have been prefent.
Some of our offerings are eaten with
bitter herbs. We had a faying among us
to any one of a crofs temper, ' That
' if they were to be eaten, they fhould
' be eaten with bitter herbs.'

We practifed circumcifion like the
Jews, and made offerings and feafts
on that occafion in the fame manner
as they did. Like them alfo, our
children

children were named from fome event, fome circumftance, or fancied foreboding at the time of their birth. I was named *Olaudah*, which, in our language, fignifies viciffitude, or fortunate alfo; one favoured, and having a loud voice and well fpoken. I remember we never polluted the name of the object of our adoration; on the contrary, it was always mentioned with the greateft reverence; and we were totally unacquainted with fwearing, and all thofe terms of abufe and reproach which find their way fo readily and copioufly into the language of more civilized people. The only expreffions of that kind I remember were, ' May you rot, or ' may you fwell, or may a beaft take ' you.'

I have before remarked that the natives of this part of Africa are extremely cleanly. This neceffary habit

of

of decency was with us a part of religion, and therefore we had many purifications and washings; indeed almoft
as many, and ufed en the fame occafions, if my recollection does not fail
me, as the Jews. Thofe that touched
the dead at any time were obliged to
wafh and purify themfelves before they
could enter a dwelling-houfe. Every woman too, at certain times, was foi bidden
to come into a dwelling-houfe, or touch
any perfon, or any thing we eat. I was
fo fond of my mother I could not keep
from her, or avoid touching her at
fome of thofe periods, in confequenee
of which I was obliged to be kept
out with her, in a little houfe made for
that purpofe, till offering was made,
and then we were purified.

Though we had no places of public worfhip, we had priefts and magicians, or wife men. I do not remember

ber whether they had different offices, or whether they were united in the same persons, but they were held in great reverence by the people. They calculated our time, and foretold events, as their name imported, for we called them Ah-affoe-way-cah, which signifies calculators or yearly men, our year being called Ah-affoe. They wore their beards, and when they died they were suceeded by their sons. Most of their implements and things of value were interred along with them. Pipes and tobacco were also put into the grave with the corpse, which was always perfumed and ornamented, and animals were offered in sacrifice to them. None accompanied their funerals but those of the same profession or tribe. These buried them after sunset, and always returned from the grave by

C 5   a different

a different way from that which they
went.

These magicians were also our doctors or physicians. They practised bleed-
ing by cupping; and were very success-
ful in healing wounds and expelling
poisons. They had likewise some extraordinary method of discovering jea-
lousy, theft, and poisoning; the success
of which no doubt they derived from
the unbounded influence over the
credulity and superstition of the people.
I do not remember what those methods
were, except that as to poisoning. I
recollect an instance or two, which I
hope it will not be deemed impertinent
here to insert, as it may serve as a kind
of specimen of the rest, and is still
used by the negroes in the West Indies.
A young woman had been poisoned, but
it was not known by whom: the doctor
ordered the corpse to be taken up by
some

some persons, and carried to the grave. As soon as the bearers had raised it on their shoulders, they seemed seized with some * sudden impulse, and ran to and fro unable to stop themselves. At last, after having passed through a number of thorns and prickly bushes, unhurt, the corpse fell from them close to a house, and defaced it in the fall; and the owner being taken up, he immediately confessed the poisoning †.

The

* See also Lieut. Matthew's Voyage, p. 123.

† An instance of this kind happened at Montserrat in the West Indies in the year 1763. I then belonged to the Charming Sally, Capt. Doran — The chief mate, Mr Mansfield, and some of the crew being one day on shore, were present at the burying of a poisoned negro girl. Though they had often heard of the circumstance of the running in such cases, and had even seen it, they imagined it to be a trick of the corpse-bearers. They were therefore desired two of the sailors to take up the coffin, and carry it to the grave. The sailors, who were all of the same opinion, readily obeyed but they had scarcely raised it to their shoulders, before

The natives are extremely cautious about poifon. When they buy any eatable the feller kiffes it all round before the buyer, to fhew him it is not poifoned; and the fame is done when any meat or drink is prefented, particularly to a ftranger. We have ferpents of different kinds, fome of which are efteemed ominous when they appear in our houfes, and thefe we never moleft. I remember two of thofe ominous fnakes, each of which was as thick as the calf of a man's leg, and in colour refembling a dolphin in the water, crept at different times into my

about, quite unable to direct themfelves, till, at laft, without intention, they came to the hut of him who had poifoned the girl. The coffin then immediately fell from their fhoulders againft the hut, and damaged part of the wall. The owner of the hut was taken into cuftody on this, and con feffed the poifoning.—I give this ftory as it was related by the mate and crew on their return to the fhip. The credit which is due to it I leave with the reader.

mother's

mother's night-houfe, where I always lay with her, and coiled themfelves into folds, and each time they crowed like a cock. I was defired by fome of our wife men to touch thefe, that I might be interefted in the good omens, which I did, for they were quite harm-lefs, and would tamely fuffer them-felves to be handled; and then they were put into a large open earthen pan, and fet on one fide of the high-way. Some of our fnakes, however, were poifonous: one of them croffed the road one day as I was ftanding on it, and paffed between my feet without offering to touch me, to the great furprife of many who faw it; and thefe incidents were accounted by the wife men, and likewife by my mother and the reft of the people, as remark-able omens in my favour.

Such is the imperfect fketch my memory.

memory has furnished me with of the manners and cuftoms of a people among whom I firft drew my breath. And here I cannot forbear fuggefting what has long ftruck me very forcibly, namely, the ftrong analogy which even by this fketch, imperfect as it is, appears to prevail in the manners and cuftoms of my countrymen and thofe of the Jews, before they reached the Land of Promife, and particularly the patriarchs while they were yet in that paftoral ftate which is defcribed in Genefis—an analogy, which alone would induce me to think that the one people had fprung from the other. Indeed this is the opinion of Dr. Gill, who, in his commentary on Genefis, very ably deduces the pedigree of the Africans from Afer and Afra, the defcendants of Abraham by Keturah his wife and concubine (for both thefe titles are

applied

applied to her). It is also conformable
to the fentiments of Dr. John Clarke,
formerly Dean of Sarum, in his Truth
of the Chriſtian Religion: both theſe
authors concur in aſcribing to us this
original. The reaſonings of thoſe gentlemen are ſtill further confirmed by
the ſcripture chronology; and if any
further corroboration were required,
this reſemblance in ſo many reſpects
is a ſtrong evidence in ſupport of
the opinion. Like the Iſraelites in
their primitive ſtate, our government
was conducted by our chiefs or judges,
our wiſe men and elders; and the head
of a family with us enjoyed a ſimilar
authority over his houſehold with that
which is aſcribed to Abraham and the
other patriarchs. The law of retaliation obtained almoſt univerſally with us
as with them. and even their religion
appeared to have ſhed upon us a ray of

its

its glory, though broken and spent in its passage, or eclipsed by the cloud with which time, tradition, and ignorance might have enveloped it; for we had our circumcision (a rule I believe peculiar to that people·) we had also our sacrifices and burnt-offerings, our washings and purifications, on the same occasions as they had.

As to the difference of colour between the Eboan Africans and the modern Jews, I shall not presume to account for it. It is a subject which has engaged the pens of men of both genius and learning, and is far above my strength. The most able and Reverend Mr. T. Clarkson, however, in his much admired Essay on the Slavery and Commerce of the Human Species, has ascertained the cause in a manner that at once solves every objection on that account, and, on my mind at least,

has

has produced the fulleſt conviction. I ſhall therefore refer to that perform- ance for the theory *, contenting my- ſelf with extricating a fact as related by Dr. Mitchel †. " The Spaniards, " who have inhabited America, under " the torrid zone, for any time, are " become as dark coloured as our na- " tive Indians of Virginia ; of which " *I myſelf have been a witneſs.*" There is alſo another inſtance ‡ of a Portugueſe ſettlement at Mitomba, a river in Sierra Leona ; where the inhabitants are bred from a mixture of the firſt Portugueſe diſcoverers with the natives, and are now become in their complexion, and in the woolly quality of their

* Page 178 to 216.
† Philoſ. Tranſ. No. 476, Sect. 4, cited by Mr Clarkſon, p. 205.
‡ Same page.

hair.

hair, *perfect negroes*, retaining however a smattering of the Portuguese
language.

These instances, and a great many
more which might be adduced, while
they shew how the complexions of the
same persons vary in different climates
it is hoped may tend also to remove
the prejudice that some conceive against
the natives of Africa on account of
their colour. Surely the minds of the
Spaniards did not change with their
complexions! Are there not causes
enough to which the apparent infe-
riority of an African may be ascribed
without limiting the goodness of God
and supposing he forbore to stamp un-
derstanding on certainly his own image
because " carved in ebony." Might
it not naturally be ascribed to their
situation? When they come among
Europeans, they are ignorant of their
                                    language,

language, religion, manners, and cuſtoms. Are any pains taken to teach them theſe? Are they treated as men? Does not ſlavery itſelf depreſs the mind, and extinguiſh all its fire and every noble ſentiment? But, above all, what advantages do not a refined people poſſeſs over thoſe who are rude and uncultivated. Let the poliſhed and haughty European recollect that *his* anceſtors were once, like the Africans, uncivilized, and even barbarous. Did Nature make *them* inferior to their ſons? and ſhould *they too* have been made ſlaves? Every rational mind anſwers, No. Let ſuch reflections as theſe melt the pride of their ſuperiority into ſympathy for the wants and miſeries of their ſable brethren, and compel them to acknowledge, that underſtanding is not confined to feature or colour. If, when they look round the

world,

world, they feel exultation, let it be tempered with benevolence to others, and gratitude to God, " who hath " made of one blood all nations of " men for to dwell on all the face of " the earth *; and whofe wifdom is " not our wifdom, neither are our " ways his ways."

* Acts xvii, 26.

CHAP.

C H A P. II.

The author's birth and parentage—His being kidnapped with his sister—Their separation—Surprise at meeting again—Are finally separated—Account of the different places and incidents the author met with till his arrival on the coast—The effect the sight of a slave ship had on him—He sails for the West Indies—Horrors of a slave ship—Arrives at Barbadoes, where the cargo is sold and dispersed.

I HOPE the reader will not think I have trespassed on his patience in introducing myself to him with some account of the manners and customs of my country. They had been im-

planted

planted in me with great care, and made an impreffion on my mind, which time could not erafe, and which all the adverfity and variety of fortune I have fince experienced, ferved only to rivet and record; for, whether the love of one's country be real or imaginary, or a leffon of reafon, or an inftinct of nature, I ftill look back with pleafure on the firft fcenes of my life, though that pleafure has been for the moft part mingled with forrow.

I have already acquainted the reader with the time and place of my birth. My father, befides many flaves, had a numerous family, of which feven lived to grow up, including myfelf and a fifter, who was the only daughter. As I was the youngeft of the fons, I became, of courfe, the greateft favourite with my mother, and was always with her, and fhe ufed to take particular

pains

pains to form my mind. I was trained up from my earlieft years in the art of war. my daily exercife was fhooting and throwing javelins; and my mother adorned me with emblems, after the manner of our greateft warriors. In this way I grew up till I was turned the age of eleven, when an end was put to my happinefs in the following manner:— Generally when the grown people in the neighbourhood were gone far in the fields to labour the children affembled together in fome of the neighbours' premifes to play, and commonly fome of us ufed to get up a tree to look out for any affailant, or kidnapper, that might come upon us, for they fometimes took thofe opportunities of our parents abfence to attack and carry off as many as they could feize. One day, as I was watching at the top of a tree in our yard, I faw one of thofe people

come

come into the yard of our next neighbour but one, to kidnap, there being
many ftout young people in it. Immediately on this I gave the alarm of the
rogue, and he was furrounded by the
ftouteft of them, who entangled him
with cords, fo that he could not efcape
till fome of the grown people came
and fecured him. But alas! ere long it
was my fate to be thus attacked, and
to be carried off, when none of the
grown people were nigh. One day,
when all our people were gone out to
their works as ufual, and only I and
my dear fifter were left to mind the
houfe, two men and a woman got over
our walls, and in a moment feized us
both, and, without giving us time to cry
out, or make refiftance, they ftopped
our mouths, and ran off with us, into
the neareft wood. Here they tied our
hands, and continued to carry us as

2   far

far as they could, till night came on,
when we reached a small house, where
the robbers halted for refreshment
and spent the night. We were then
unbound, but were unable to take any
food; and, being quite overpowered
by fatigue and grief, our only relief
was some sleep, which allayed our
misfortune for a short time. The next
morning we left the house, and continued travelling all the day. For a
long time we had kept the woods, but
at last we came into a road which I
believed I knew. I had now some
hopes of being delivered, for we had
advanced but a little way before I difcovered some people at a diftance, on
which I began to cry out for their affiftance, but my cries had no other
effect than to make them tie me faster
and ftop my mouth, and then they
put me into a large fack. They also

stopped my sister's mouth, and tied her hands; and in this manner we proceeded till we were out of the sight of these people. When we went to rest the following night they offered us some victuals; but we refused it; and the only comfort we had was in being in one another's arms all that night, and bathing each other with our tears. But alas! we were soon deprived of even the small comfort of weeping together. The next day proved a day of greater sorrow than I had yet experienced, for my sister and I were then separated, while we lay clasped in each others arms. It was in vain that we besought them not to part us; she was torn from me, and immediately carried away, while I was left in a state of distraction not to be described. I cried and grieved continually; and for several days did not eat any thing but what they forced into my mouth. At length, after many days travelling, during which I had often changed masters, I got into the hands of a chieftain, in a very pleasant country. This man had two wives and some children, and they all used me extremely well, and did all they could to comfort me; particularly the first wife, who was something like my mother. Although I was a great many days journey from my father's house, yet these people spoke exactly the same language with us. This first master of mine, as I may call him, was a smith, and my principal employment was working his bellows, which were the same kind as I had seen in my vicinity. They were in some respects not unlike the stoves here in gentlemen's kitchens; and were covered over with leather, and in the

middle

middle of that leather a stick was
fixed, and a person stood up, and
worked it, in the same manner as is
done to pump water out of a cask with
a hand pump. I believe it was gold
he worked, for it was of a lovely
bright yellow colour, and was worn
by the women on their wrists and
ancles. I was there I suppose about a
month, and they at last used to trust
me some little distance from the house.
This liberty I used in embracing every
opportunity to inquire the way to my
own home and I also sometimes, for the
same purpose, went with the maidens,
in the cool of the evenings, to bring
pitchers of water from the springs for
the use of the house. I had also remarked where the sun rose in the morning, and set in the evening, as I had
travelled along; and I had observed
that n father's house was towards the
rising

rifing of the fun. I therefore determined to feize the firft opportunity of
making my efcape, and to fhape my
courfe for that quarter, for I was quite
oppreffed and weighed down by grief
after my mother and friends; and
my love of liberty, ever great, was
ftrengthened by the mortifying circumftance of not daring to eat with
the free-born children, although I was
moftly their companion. While I was
projecting my efcape, one day an un-
lucky event happened, which quite
difconcerted my plan, and put an end
to my hopes. I ufed to be fometimes
employed in affifting an elderly woman
flave, to cook and take care of the
poultry: and one morning, while I was
feeding fome chickens, I happened to
tofs a fmall pebble at one of them,
which hit it on the middle, and directly killed it. The old flave, having

D 3   foon

foon after miffed the chicken, inquired after it ; and on my relating the accident (for I told her the truth, becaufe my mother would never fuffer me to tell a lie) fhe flew into a violent paffion, threatened that I fhould fuffer for it, and, my mafter being out, fhe immediately went and told her miftrefs what I had done. This alarmed me very much, and I expected an inftant flogging, which to me was uncommonly dreadful ; for I had feldom been beaten at home. I therefore refolved to fly ; and accordingly I ran into a thicket that was hard by, and hid myfelf in the bufhes. Soon afterwards my miftrefs and the flave returned; and, not feeing me, they fearched all the houfe, but not finding me, and I not making anfwer when they called to me, they thought I ad run away, and the whole neighbourhood

bourhood was raifed in the purfuit of me. In that part of the country (as in ours) the houfes and villages were fkirted with woods, or fhrubberies, and the bufhes were fo thick that a man could readily conceal himfelf in them, fo as to elude the ftricteft fearch. The neighbours continued the whole day looking for me, and feveral times many of them came within a few yards of the place where I lay hid. I expected every moment, when I heard a ruftling among the trees, to be found out, and punifhed by my mafter · but they never difcovered me, though they were often fo near that I even heard their conjectures as they were looking about for me; and I now learned from them, that any attempt to return home would be hopelefs. Moft of them fuppofed I had fled towards home;

but

but the diftance was fo great, and the
way fo intricate, that they thought I
could never reach it, and that I fhould
be loft in the woods. When I heard
this I was feized with a violent panic,
and abandoned myfelf to defpair.
Night too began to approach, and aggravated all my fears. I had before
entertained hopes of getting home;
and had determined when it fhould
be dark to make the attempt; but I
was now convinced it was fruitlefs,
and began to confider that, if poffibly
I could efcape all other animals, I
could not thofe of the human kind;
and that, not knowing the way, I muft
perifh in the woods. Thus was I like
the hunted deer:

 ——" Ev'ry leaf and ev'ry whifp'ring breath
 " Convey'd a foe, and ev'ry foe a death."

I heard frequent ruftlings among the
leaves, and being pretty fure they were
        fnakes.

snakes, I expected every instant to be stung by them. This increased my anguish, and the horror of my situation became now quite insupportable. I at length quitted the thicket, very faint and hungry, for I had not eaten or drank any thing all the day; and crept to my master's kitchen, from whence I set out at first, and which was an open shed, and laid myself down in the ashes with an anxious wish for death to relieve me from all my pains. I was scarcely awake in the morning, when the old woman slave, who was the first up, came to light the fire, and saw me in the fire place. She was very much surprised to see me, and could scarcely believe her own eyes. She now promised to intercede for me, and went for her master, who soon after came, and, having slightly reprimanded

me,

me, ordered me to be taken care of, and not ill treated.

Soon after this my mafter's only daughter, and child by his firft wife, fickened and died, which affected him fo much that for fome time he was almoft frantic, and really would have killed himfelf, had he not been watched and prevented. However, in a fmall time afterwards he recovered, and I was again fold. I was now carried to the left of the fun's rifing, through many dreary waftes and difmal woods, amidft the hideous roarings of wild beafts. The people I was fold to ufed to carry me very often, when I was tired, either on their fhoulders or on their backs. I faw many convenient well-built fheds along the road, at proper diftances, to accommodate the merchants and travellers, who lay in thofe buildings along with
their

their wives, who often accompany them; and they always go well armed.

From the time I left my own nation I always found somebody that understood me till I came to the sea coast. The languages of different nations did not totally differ, nor were they so copious as those of the Europeans, particularly the English. They were therefore easily learned, and, while I was journeying thus through Africa, I acquired two or three different tongues. In this manner I had been travelling for a considerable time, when one evening to my great surprise, whom should I see brought to the house where I was but my dear sister! As soon as she saw me she gave a loud shriek, and ran into my arms—I was quite overpowered: neither of us could speak; but, for a considerable time,

D 6   clung

clung to each other in mutual embraces,
unable to do any thing but weep. Our
meeting affected all who faw us; and
indeed I muft acknowledge, in honour
of thofe fable deftroyers of human
rights, that I never met with any ill
treatment, or faw any offered to their
flaves, except tying them, when neceffary, to keep them from running
away. When thefe people knew we
were brother and fifter, they indulged us
to be together; and the man, to whom I
fuppofed we belonged, lay with us, he
in the middle, while fhe and I held one
another by the hands acrofs his breaft
all night; and thus for a while we
forgot our misfortunes in the joy of
being together: but even this fmall
comfort was foon to have an end; for
fcarcely had the fatal morning appeared, when fhe was again torn from me
for 'ever! I was now more miferable,

if

if poſſible, than before. The ſmall relief which her preſence gave me from pain was gone, and the wretchedneſs of my ſituation was redoubled by my anxiety after her fate, and my apprehenſions leſt her ſufferings ſhould be greater than mine, when I could not be with her to alleviate them. Yes, thou dear partner of all my childiſh ſports! thou ſharer of my joys and ſorrows! happy ſhould I have ever eſteemed myſelf to encounter every miſery for you, and to procure your freedom by the ſacrifice of my own. Though you were early forced from my arms, your image has been always rivetted in my heart, from which neither *time nor fortune* have been able to remove it; ſo that, while the thoughts of your ſufferings have damped my proſperity, they have mingled with adverſity and increaſed its bitterneſs.

To

To that Heaven which protects the weak from the strong, I commit the care of your innocence and virtues, if they have not already received their full reward, and if your youth and delicacy have not long since fallen victims to the violence of the African trader, the pestilential stench of a Guinea ship, the seasoning in the European colonies, or the lash and lust of a brutal and unrelenting overseer.

I did not long remain after my sister. I was again sold, and carried through a number of places, till, after travelling a considerable time, I came to a town called Tinmah, in the most beautiful country I had yet seen in Africa. It was extremely rich, and there were many rivulets which flowed through it, and supplied a large pond in the centre of the town, where the people washed. Here I first saw and tasted cocoa nuts,

which

which I thought fuperior to any nuts I
had ever tafted before; and the trees,
which were loaded, were alfo interfperf-
ed amongft the houfes, which had commodious fhades adjoining, and were
in the fame manner as ours, the infides
being neatly plaftered and whitewafhed,
Here I alfo faw and tafted for the firft
time fugar-cane. Their money confifted
of little white fhells, the fize of the fin-
ger nail. I was fold here for one hundred
and feventy-two of them by a merchant
who lived and brought me there. I
had been about two or three days at
his houfe, when a wealthy widow, a
neighbour of his, came there one evening, and brought with her an only
fon, a young gentleman about my own
age and fize. Here they faw me; and,
having taken a fancy to me, I was
bought of the merchant, and went
home with them. Her houfe and
premifes

premises were situated close to one of
those rivulets I have mentioned, and
were the finest I ever saw in Africa:
they were very extensive, and she had
a number of slaves to attend her. The
next day I was washed and perfumed,
and when meal-time came, I was led
into the presence of my mistress, and
eat and drank before her with her son.
This filled me with astonishment; and
I could scarce help expressing my surprise that the young gentleman should
suffer me, who was bound, to eat with
him who was free; and not only so,
but that he would not at any time either
eat or drink till I had taken first, because I was the eldest, which was
agreeable to our custom. Indeed every
thing here, and all their treatment of
me, made me forget that I was a slave.
The language of these people resembled ours so nearly, that we understood
each

each other perfectly. They had alfo the very fame cuftoms as we. There were likewife flaves daily to attend us, while my young mafter and I with other boys fported with our darts and bows and arrows, as I had been ufed to do at home. In this refemblance to my former happy ftate, I paffed about two months; and I now began to think I was to be adopted into the family, and was beginning to be reconciled to my fituation, and to forget by degrees my misfortunes, when all at once the delufion vanifhed; for, without the leaft previous knowledge, one morning early, while my dear mafter and companion was ftill afleep, I was awakened out of my reverie to frefh forrow, and hurried away even amongft the uncircumcifed.

Thus, at the very moment I dreamed of the greateft happinefs, I found myfelf

self most miserable; and it seemed as it
fortune wished to give me this taste of
joy, only to render the reverse more
poignant. The change I now experienced was as painful as it was sudden
and unexpected. It was a change indeed from a state of bliss to a scene
which is inexpressible by me, as it
discovered to me an element I had
never before beheld, and till then had
no idea of, and wherein such instances
of hardship and cruelty continually oc-
curred as I can never reflect on but
with horror.

All the nations and people I had
hitherto passed through resembled our
own in their manners, customs, and
language: but I came at length to
a country, the inhabitants of which
differed from us in all those particulars.
I was very much struck with this difference, especially when I came among
a people

a people who did not circumcise, and
eat without washing their hands. They
cooked also in iron pots, and had European cutlaffes and crofs bows, which
were unknown to us, and fought with
their fifts amongft themfelves. Their
women were not fo modeft as ours,
for they eat, and drank, and flept,
with their men. But above all, I was
amazed to fee no facrifices or offerings
among them. In fome of thofe places
the people ornamented themfelves with
fcars, and likewife filed their teeth
very fharp. They wanted fometimes
to ornament me in the fame manner,
but I would not fuffer them; hoping
that I might fome time be among a
people who did not thus disfigure themfelves, as I thought they did. At laft
I came to the banks of a large river,
which was covered with canoes, in
which the people appeared to live

with

with their houfehold utenfils and provifions of all kinds. I was beyond
meafure aftonifhed at this, as I had
never before feen any water larger than
a pond or a rivulet : and my furprife
was mingled with no fmall fear when
I was put into one of thefe canoes,
and we began to paddle and move
along the river. We continued going
on thus till night; and when we came
to land, and made fires on the banks,
each family by themfelves, fome dragged
their canoes on fhore, others ftayed and
cooked in theirs, and laid in them all
night. Thofe on the land had mats,
of which they made tents, fome in the
fhape of little houfes : in thefe we flept :
and after the morning meal, we em-
barked again and proceeded as before.
I was often very much aftonifhed to
fee fome of the women, as well as the
men, jump into the water, dive to the
bottom,

bottom, come up again, and fwim about. Thus I continued to travel, fometimes by land, fometimes by water, through different countries and various nations, till, at the end of fix or feven months after I had been kidnapped, I arrived at the fea coaft. It would be tedious and uninterefting to relate all the incidents which befell me during this journey, and which I have not yet forgotten; of the various hands I paffed through, and the manners and cuftoms of all the different people among whom I lived: I fhall therefore only obferve, that in all the places where I was, the foil was exceedingly rich; the pomkins, aedas, plantains, yams, &c. &c. were in great abundance, and of incredible fize. There were alfo vaft quantities of different gums, though not ufed for any purpofe, and every where a great deal of tobacco.

tobacco. The cotton even grew quite wild, and there was plenty of red-wood. I saw no mechanics whatever in all the way, except such as I have mentioned. The chief employment in all these countries was agriculture, and both the males and females, as with us, were brought up to it, and trained in the arts of war.

The first object which saluted my eyes when I arrived on the coast was the sea, and a slave ship, which was then riding at anchor, and waiting for its cargo. These filled me with astonishment, which was soon converted into terror when I was carried on board. I was immediately handled, and tossed up to see if I were sound, by some of the crew; and I was now persuaded that I had gotten into a world of bad spirits, and that they were going to kill me. Their complexions too

differing

differing so much from ours, their long
hair, and the language they spoke,
(which was very different from any I
had ever heard) united to confirm me
in this belief. Indeed such were the
horrors of my views and fears at the
moment, that, if ten thousand worlds
had been my own, I would have freely
parted with them all to have exchanged
my condition with that of the meanest
slave in my own country. When I looked round the ship too and saw a large
furnace or copper boiling, and a mul-
titude of black people of every descrip-
tion chained together, every one of
their countenances expressing dejection
and sorrow, I no longer doubted of
my fate; and, quite overpowered with
horror and anguish, I fell motionless
on the deck and fainted. When I
recovered a little I found some black
people about me, who I believed were

some

fome of thofe who brought me on board, and had been receiving their pay; they talked to me in order to cheer me, but all in vain. I afked them if we were not to be eaten by thofe white men with horrible looks, red faces, and long hair. They told me I was not: and one of the crew brought me a fmall portion of fpirituous liquor in a wine glafs; but, being afraid of him, I would not take it out of his hand. One of the blacks therefore took it from him and gave it to me, and I took a little down my palate, which, inftead of reviving me, as they thought it would, threw me into the greateft confternation at the ftrange feeling it produced, having never tafted any fuch liquor before. Soon after this the blacks who brought me on board went off, and left me abandoned to defpair. I now faw myfelf deprived

of

of all chance of returning to my native
country, or even the least glimpse of
hope of gaining the shore, which I now
considered as friendly; and I even
wished for my former slavery in preference to my present situation, which
was filled with horrors of every kind,
still heightened by my ignorance of
what I was to undergo. I was not
long suffered to indulge my grief; I
was soon put down under the decks,
and there I received such a salutation
in my nostrils as I had never experienced in my life: so that, with the
loathsomeness of the stench, and crying
together, I became so sick and low
that I was not able to eat, nor had I
the least desire to taste any thing. I
now wished for the last friend, death,
to relieve me; but soon, to my grief,
two of the white men offered me eat-
ables; and, on my refusing to eat,

one of them held me fast by the hands, and laid me acrofs, I think the windlafs, and tied my feet, while the other flogged me feverely. I had never experienced any thing of this kind before; and although not being ufed to the water, I naturally feared that element the firft time I faw it, yet neverthelefs, could I have got over the nettings, I would have jumped over the fide, but I could not; and, befides, the crew ufed to watch us very clofely who were not chained down to the decks, left we fhould leap into the water: and I have feen fome of thefe poor African prifoners moft feverely cut for attempting to do fo, and hourly whipped for not eating. This indeed was often the cafe with myfelf. In a little time after, amongft the poor chained men, I found fome of my own nation, which in a fmall degree gave eafe to my mind. I

inquired

inquired of thefe what was to be done with us? they gave me to underftand we were to be carried to thefe white people's country to work for them. I then was a little revived, and thought, if it were no worfe than working, my fituation was not fo defperate: but ftill I feared I fhould be put to death, the white people looked and acted, as I thought, in fo favage a manner; for I had never feen among any people fuch inftances of brutal cruelty; and this not only fhewn towards us blacks, but alfo to fome of the whites themfelves. One white man in particular I faw, when we were permitted to be on deck, flogged fo unmercifully with a large rope near the foremaft, that he died in confequence of it; and they toffed him over the fide as they would have done a brute. This made me fear thefe people the more; and I ex-

E 2

pected

pected nothing lefs than to be treated in the fame manner. I could not help expreffing my fears and apprehenfions to fome of my countrymen · I afked them if thefe people had no country, but lived in this hollow place (the fhip)? they told me they did not, but came from a diftant one. ' Then,' faid I, ' how comes it in all our country we ' never heard of them?' They told me becaufe they lived fo very far off. I then afked where were their women? had they any like themfelves? I was told they had: ' And why,' faid I, ' do we ' not fee them?' they anfwered, becaufe they were left behind. I afked how the veffel could go? they told me they could not tell; but that there were cloth put upon the mafts by the help of the ropes I faw, and then the veffel went on; and the white men had fome fpell or magic they put in the water when

when they liked in order to ftop the veffel. I was exceedingly amazed at this account, and really thought they were fpirits. I therefore wifhed much to be from amongft them, for I expected they would facrifice me but my wifhes were vain; for we were fo quartered that it was impoffible for any of us to make our efcape. While we ftayed on the coaft I was moftly on deck, and one day, to my great aftonifhment, I faw one of thefe veffels coming in with the fails up. As foon as the whites faw it, they gave a great fhout, at which we were amazed; and the more fo as the veffel appeared larger by approaching nearer. At laft fhe came to an anchor in my fight, and when the anchor was let go I and my countrymen who faw it were loft in aftonifhment to obferve the veffel ftop; and were now convinced it was

E 3   done

done by magic. Soon after this 'the other fhip got her boats out, and they came on board of us, and the people of both fhips feemed very glad to fee each other. Several of the ftrangers alfo fhook hands with us black people, and made motions with their hands, fignifying I fuppofe, we were to go to their country; but we did not underftand them. At laft, when the fhip we were in, had got in all her cargo, they made ready with many fearful noifes, and we were all put under deck, fo that we could not fee how they managed the veffel. But this difappointment was the leaft of my forrow. The ftench of the hold while we were on the coaft was fo intolerably loathfome, that it was dangerous to remain there for any time, and fome of us had been permitted to ftay on the deck for the frefh air; but now that the whole fhip's cargo were

confined

confined together, it became abfolutely
peftilential. The clofenefs of the place,
and the heat of the climate, added to
the number in the fhip, which was fo
crowded that each had fcarcely room
to turn himfelf, almoft fuffocated us.
This produced copious perfpirations,
fo that the air foon became unfit for
refpiration, from a variety of loathfome fmells, and brought on a ficknefs
among the flaves, of which many died,
thus falling victims to the improvident
avarice, as I may call it, of their pur-
chafers. This wretched fituation was
again aggravated by the galling of the
chains, now become infupportable;
and the filth of the neceffary tubs, into
which the children often fell, and were
almoft fuffocated. The fhrieks of the
women, and the groans of the dying,
rendered the whole a fcene of horror
almoft inconceivable. Happily perhaps

E 4   for

for myfelf I was foon reduced fo low here that it was thought neceffary to keep me almoft always on-deck, and from my extreme youth I was not put in fetters. In this fituation I expected every hour to fhare the fate of my companions, fome of whom were al-moft daily brought upon deck at the point of death, which I began to hope would foon put an end to my miferies. Often did I think many of the inhabitants of the deep much more happy than myfelf, I envied them the freedom they enjoyed, and as often wifhed I could change my condition for theirs. Every circumftance I met with ferved only to render my ftate more painful, and heighten my apprehenfions, and my opinion of the cruelty of the whites. One day they had taken a number of fifhes; and when they had killed and fatisfied themfelves with as many as

they

they thought fit, to our astonishment who were on the deck, rather than give any of them to us to eat, as we expected, they tossed the remaining fish into the sea again, although we begged and prayed for some as well as we could, but in vain; and some of my countrymen, being pressed by hunger, took an opportunity, when they thought no one saw them, of trying to get a little privately; but they were discovered, and the attempt procured them some very severe floggings. One day, when we had a smooth sea and moderate wind, two of my wearied countrymen who were chained together (I was near them at the time), preferring death to such a life of misery, somehow made through the nettings and jumped into the sea: immediately another quite dejected fellow, who on account of his illness, was suffered to be out of irons,

E 5   also

alfo followed their example; and I believe many more would very foon have
done the fame if they had not been prevented by the fhip's crew, who were
inftantly alarmed. Thofe of us that
were the moft active were in a moment
put down under the deck, and there
was fuch a noife and confufion amongft
the people of the fhip as I never heard
before, to ftop her, and get the boat
out to go after the flaves. However
two of the wretches were drowned, but
they got the other, and afterwards
flogged him unmercifully, for thus attempting to prefer death to flavery.
In this manner we continued to undergo more hardfhips than I can now
relate, hardfhips which are infeparable
from this accurfed trade. Many a
time we were near fuffocation from the
want of frefh air, which we were often
without for whole days together. This,
and

and the ftench of the neceffary tubs, carried off many. During our paffage I firft faw flying fifhes, which furprifed me very much: they ufed frequently to fly acrofs the fhip, and many of them fell on the deck. I alfo now firft faw the ufe of the quadrant; I had often with aftonifhment feen the mariners make obfervations with it, and I could not think what it meant. They at laft took notice of my furprife: and one of them, willing to increafe it, as well as to giatify my curiofity, made me one day look through it. The clouds appeared to me to be land, which difappeared as they paffed along. This heightened my wonder; and I was now more perfuaded than ever that I was in another world, and that every thing about me was magic. At laft we came in fight of the ifland of Barbadoes, at which the whites on board gave a great

E 6   fhout,

shout, and made many signs of joy to us. We did not know what to think of this, but as the vessel drew nearer we plainly saw the harbour, and other ships of different kinds and sizes, and we soon anchored amongst them off Bridge Town. Many merchants and planters now came on board, though it was in the evening. They put us in separate parcels, and examined us attentively. They also made us jump, and pointed to the land, signifying we were to go there. We thought by this we should be eaten by these ugly men, as they appeared to us; and, when soon after we were all put down under the deck again, there was much dread and trembling among us, and nothing but bitter cries to be heard all the night from these apprehensions, insomuch that at last the white people got some old slaves from the land to pacify us. They

told

told us we were not to be eaten, but
to work, and were foon to go on land,
where we fhould fee many of our
country people. This report eafed us
much, and fure enough, foon after
we were landed, there came to us
Africans of all languages. We were
conducted immediately to the merchant's yard, where we were all pent
up together like fo many fheep in a
fold, without regard to fex or age. As
every object was new to me every thing
I faw filled me with furprife. What
ftruck me firft was that the houfes were
built with bricks and ftories, and in every
other refpect different from thofe I had
feen in Africa: but I was ftill more aftonifhed on feeing people on horfeback.
I did not know what this could mean;
and indeed I thought thefe people were
full of nothing but magical arts. While
I was in this aftonifhment one of my
fellow

fellow prifoners fpoke to a countryman of his about the horfes, who faid they were the fame kind they had in their country. I underftood them, though they were from a diftant part of Afiica, and I thought it odd I had not feen any horfes there; but afterwards, when I came to converfe with different Africans, I found they had many horfes amongft them, and much laiger than thofe I then faw. We were not many days in the merchant's cuftody before we were fold after their ufual manner, which is this:—On a fignal given, (as the beat of a drum) the buyers rufh at once into the yard where the flaves are confined, and make choice of that parcel they like beft. The noife and clamour with which this is attended, and the eagernefs vifible in the countenances of the buyers, ferve not a little to increafe the apprehenfion of the

terrified

terrified Africans, who may well be
fuppofed to confider them as the mini-
fters of that deftruction to which they
think themfelves devoted. In this
manner, without fcruple, are relations
and friends feparated, moft of them
never to fee each other again. I remember in the veffel in which I was
brought over, in the men's apartment,
there were feveral brothers, who, in the
fale, were fold in different lots; and it
was very moving on this occafion to
fee and hear their cries at parting. O,
ve nominal Chriftians! might not an
African afk you, learned you this
from your God, who fays unto you,
Do unto all men as you would men
fhould do unto you? Is it not enough
that we are torn from our country and
friends, to toil for your luxury and luft
of gain? Muft every tender feeling be
likewife facrificed to your avarice?

Are

Are the deareft friends and relations, now rendered more dear by their fepa-ration from their kindred, ftill to be parted fiom each other, and thus pre-vented from checiing the gloom of flavery with the fmall comfoit of being together and mingling their fufferings and forrows? Why are parents to lofe their children, brothers their fifters, or hufbands their wives? Surely this is a new refinement in cruelty, which, while it has no advantage to atone for it, thus aggravates diftrefs, and adds frefh horrors even to the wretchednefs of flavery.

CHAP.

C H A P. III.

The author is carried to Virginia—His dif-
trefs—Surprife at feeing a picture and
a watch—Is bought by Captain Pafcal,
and fets out for England—His terror
during the voyage—Arrives in England
—His wonder at a fall of fnow—Is
fent to Guernfey, and in fome time goes
on board a fhip of war with his mafter
—Some account of the expedition againft
Louifbourg under the command of Admi-
ral Bofcawen, in 1758.

I now totally loft the fmall remains
of comfort I had enjoyed in con-
verfing with my countrymen; the women too, who ufed to wafh and take
care of me, were all gone different
ways,

ways, and I never saw one of them
afterwards.

I stayed in this island for a few days;
I believe it could not be above a fortnight; when I and some few more
slaves, that were not saleable amongst
the rest, from very much fretting,
were shipped off in a sloop for North
America. On the passage we were
better treated than when we were coming from Africa, and we had plenty of
rice and fat pork. We were landed
up a river a good way from the sea,
about Virginia county, where we saw
few or none of our native Africans,
and not one soul who could talk to me.
I was a few weeks weeding grass, and
gathering stones in a plantation; and
at last all my companions were distri-
buted different ways, and only myself
was left. I was now exceedingly miserable, and thought myself worse off
than

than any of the reft of my companions; for they could talk to each other, but I had no perfon to fpeak to that I could underftand. In this ftate I was conftantly grieving and pining, and wifhing for death rather than any thing elfe. While I was in this plantation the gentleman, to whom I fuppofe the eftate belonged, being unwell, I was one day fent for to his dwelling houfe to fan him; when I came into the room where he was I was very much affrighted at fome things I faw, and the more fo, as I had feen a black woman flave as I came through the houfe, who was cooking the dinner, and the poor creature was cruelly loaded with various kinds of iron machines; fhe had one particularly on her head, which locked her mouth fo faft that fhe could fcarcely fpeak; and could not eat nor drink. I was much aftonifhed and fhocked at

this

this contrivance, which I afterwards learned was called the iron muzzle. Soon after I had a fan put into my hand, to fan the gentleman while he slept; and so I did indeed with great fear. While he was fast asleep I indulged myself a great deal in looking about the room, which to me appeared very fine and curious. The first object that engaged my attention was a watch which hung on the chimney, and was going. I was quite surprised at the noise it made, and was afraid it would tell the gentleman any thing I might do amifs. and when I immediately after observed a picture hanging in the room, which appeared constantly to look at me, I was still more affrighted, having never seen such things as thefe before. At one time I thought it was something relative to magic; and not feeing it move I thought it might be fome way

the

the whites had to keep their great men when they died, and offer them libations as we used to do to our friendly spirits. In this state of anxiety I remained till my master awoke, when I was dismissed out of the room, to my no small satisfaction and relief, for I thought that these people were all made up of wonders. In this place I was called Jacob, but on board the African snow I was called Michael. I had been some time in this miserable, forlorn, and much dejected state, without having any one to talk to, which made my life a burden, when the kind and unknown hand of the Creator (who in very deed leads the blind in a way they know not) now began to appear, to my comfort; for one day the captain of a merchant ship, called the Industrious Bee, came on some business to my master's house. This gentleman, whose name was Michael

chael Henry Pafcal, was a lieutenant
in the royal navy, but now commanded
this trading fhip, which was fome-
where in the confines of the county
many miles off. While he was at my
mafter's houfe it happened that he faw
me, and liked me fo well that he made
a purchafe of me. I think I have
often heard him fay he gave thirty or
forty pounds fterling for me; but I do
not now remember which. However, he
meant me for a prefent to fome of his
friends in England · and I was fent
accordingly from the houfe of my then
mafter, (one Mr. Campbell) to the
place where the fhip lay; I was conducted on horfeback by an elderly
black man, (a mode of travelling
which appeared very odd to me).
When I arrived I was carried on board
a fine large fhip, loaded with tobacco,
&c. and juft ready to fail for England.
I now

I now thought my condition much mended; I had fails to lie on, and plenty of good victuals to eat; and every body on board ufed me very kindly, quite contrary to what I had feen of any white people before; I therefore began to think that they were not all of the fame difpofition. A few days after I was on board we failed for England. I was ftill at a lofs to conjecture my deftiny. By this time, however, I could fmatter a little imperfect Englifh; and I wanted to know as well as I could where we were going. Some of the people of the fhip ufed to tell me they were going to carry me back to my own country, and this made me very happy. I was quite rejoiced at the idea of going back, and thought if I fhould get home what wonders I fhould have to tell. But I was referved for another

2   fate,

fate, and was soon undeceived, when we came within sight of the English coast. While I was on board this ship, my captain and master named me *Gustavus Vesa*. I at that time began to understand him a little, and refused to be called so, and told him as well as I could that I would be called Jacob, but he said I should not, and still called me Gustavus; and when I refused to answer to my new name, which at first I did, it gained me many a cuff; so at length I submitted, and by which I have been known ever since. The ship had a very long passage; and on that account we had very short allowance of provisions. Towards the last we had only one pound and a half of bread per week, and about the same quantity of meat, and one quart of water a-day. We spoke with only one vessel the whole time we were

at

at fea, and but once we caught a few fifhes. In our extremities the captain and people told me in jeft they would kill and eat me; but I thought them in earneft, and was depreffed beyond meafure, expecting every moment to be my laft. While I was in this fitu-ation one evening they caught, with a good deal of trouble, a large fhark, and got it on board. This glad-dened my poor heart exceedingly, as I thought it would ferve the people to eat inftead of their eating me; but very foon, to my aftonifhment, they cut off a fmall part of the tail, and toffed the reft over the fide. This renewed my confternation; and I did not know what to think of thefe white people, though I very much feared they would kill and eat me. There was on board the fhip a young lad who had never been at fea before, about

four or five years older than myself,
his name was Richard Baker. He was
a native of America, had received an ex-
cellent education, and was of a moſt
amiable temper. Soon after I went on
board he ſhewed me a great deal of
partiality and attention, and in return
I grew extremely fond of him. We
at length became inſeparable ; and,
for the ſpace of two years, he was of
very great uſe to me, and was my
conſtant companion and inſtructor.
Although this dear youth had many
ſlaves of his own, yet he and I have
gone through many ſufferings together
on ſhipboard, and we have many
nights lain in each other's boſoms when
we were in great diſtreſs. Thus ſuch
a friendſhip was cemented between us
as we cheriſhed till his death, which
to my very great ſorrow, happened in
the year 1759, when he was up the
                              Archipelago

Archipelago, on board his majesty's ship the Preston: an event which I have never ceased to regret, as I lost at once a kind interpreter, an agreeable companion, and a faithful friend; who, at the age of fifteen, discovered a mind superior to prejudice; and who was not ashamed to notice, to associate with, and to be the friend and instructor of one who was ignorant, a stranger, of a different complexion, and a slave! My master had lodged in his mother's house in America: he respected him very much, and made him always eat with him in the cabin. He used often to tell him jocularly that he would kill and eat me. Sometimes he would say to me—the black people were not good to eat, and would ask me if we did not eat people in my country. I said, No: then he said he would kill Dick (as he always called him) first,

F 2

and

and afterwards me. Though this hearing relieved my mind a little as to myself, I was alarmed for Dick, and whenever he was called I used to be very much afraid he was to be killed; and I would peep and watch to see if they were going to kill him: nor was I free from this confternation till we made the land. One night we loft a man overboard; and the cries and noife were fo great and confufed, in ftopping the fhip, that I, who did not know what was the matter, began, as ufual, to be very much afraid, and to think they were going to make an offering with me, and perform fome magic; which I ftill believed they dealt in. As the waves were very high I thought the Ruler of the feas was angry, and I expected to be offered up to appeafe him. This filled my mind with agony, and I could not any more

tha

that night clofe my eyes again to reft. However, when daylight appeared was a little eafed in my mind; but ftill every time I was called I ufed to think it was to be killed. Some time after this we faw fome very large fifh, which I afterwards found were called grampuffes. They looked to me extremely terrible, and made their appearance juft at dufk; and were fo near as to blow the water on the fhip's deck. I believed them to be the rulers of the fea; and as the white people did not make any offerings at any time, I thought they were angry with them: and, at laft, what confirmed my belief was, the wind juft then died away, and a calm enfued, and in confequence of it the fhip ftopped going. I fuppofed that the fifh had performed this, and I hid myfelf in the fore part of the fhip, through fear of be-

F 3

ing

ing offered up to appeafe them, every minute peeping and quaking. but my good friend Dick came fhortly towards me, and I took an opportunity to afk him, as well as I could, what thefe fifh were. Not being able to talk much Englifh, I could but juft make him underftand my queftion, and not at all, when I afked him if any offerings were to be made to them however, he told me thefe fifh would fwallow any body; which fufficiently alarmed me. Here he was called away by the captain, who was leaning over the quarter-deck railing and looking at the fifh, and moft of the people were bufied in getting a barrel of pitch to light, for them to play with. The captain now called me to him, having learned fome of my apprehenfions from Dick, and having diverted himfelf and others for fome time with my fears

which

which appeared ludicrous enough in receiving and trembling, he difmiffed me. The barrel of pitch was now lighted and put over the fide into the water by this time it was juft dark, and the fifh went after it; and, to my great joy, I faw them no more.

However, all my alarms began to fubfide when we got fight of land, and at laft the fhip arrived at Falmouth, after a paffage of thirteen weeks. Every heart on board feemed gladdened on our reaching the fhore, and none more than mine. The captain immediately went on fhore, and fent on board fome frefh provifions, which we wanted very much. we made good ufe of them, and our famine was foon turned into feafting, almoft without ending It was about the beginning of the fpring 1757, when I arrived in England, and I was near twelve years of age at that

F 4   time.

time. I was very much ftruck with the buildings and the pavement of the ftreets in Falmouth; and, indeed, every object I faw filled me with new furprife. One morning, when I got upon deck, I faw it covered all over with the fnow that fell over-night. as I had never feen any thing of the kind before, I thought it was falt, fo I immediately ran down to the mate and defired him, as well as I could, to come and fee how fomebody in the night had thrown falt all over the deck. He, knowing what it was, defired me to bring fome of it down to him: accordingly I took up a handful of it, which I found very cold indeed, and when I brought it to him he defired me to tafte it. I did fo, and I was furprifed beyond meafure. I then afked him what it was; he told me it was fnow: but I could not in anywife underftand him. He

afked

aſked me if we had no ſuch thing in
my countiy; and I told him, No
I then aſked him the uſe of it, and
who made it; he told me a great man
in the heavens, called God · but here
again I was to all intents and purpoſes
at a loſs to underſtand him; and the
more ſo, when a little after I ſaw the
air filled with it, in a heavy ſhower,
which fell down on the ſame day.
After this I went to church; and
having never been at ſuch a place
before, I was again amazed at ſeeing
and hearing the ſervice. I aſked all I
could about it; and they gave me to
underſtand it was worſhipping God,
who made us and all things. I was
ſtill at a great loſs, and ſoon got into an
endleſs field of inquiries, as well as I
was able to ſpeak and aſk about things
However, my little friend Dick uſed to

be my beft interpreter; for I could
make free with him, and he always in-
ftructed me with pleafure : and from
what I could underftand by him of this
God, and in feeing thefe white people
did not fell one another as we did, I
was much pleafed, and in this I thought
they were much happier than we Africans. I was aftonifhed at the wifdom
of the white people in all things I faw,
but was amazed at their not facrificing,
or making any offerings, and eating
with unwafhed hands, and touching the
dead. I likewife could not help re-
marking the particular flendernefs of
their women, which I did not at fuft
like, and I thought they were not fo
modeft and fhamefaced as the African
women.

I had often feen my mafter and Dick
employed in reading, and I had a
great curiofity to talk to the books, as
I thoug't

I thought they did, and fo to learn how all things had a beginning: for that purpofe I have often taken up a book, and have talked to it, and then put my ears to it, when alone, in hopes it would anfwer me, and I have been very much concerned when I found it remained filent.

My mafter lodged at the houfe of a gentleman in Falmouth, who had a fine little daughter about fix or feven years of age, and fhe grew prodigiously fond of me, infomuch that we ufed to eat together, and had fervants to wait on us. I was fo much careffed by this family that it often reminded me of the treatment I had received from my little noble African mafter. After I had been here a few days, I was fent on board of the fhip; but the child cried fo much after me that nothing could pacify her till I was fent for again.

F 6

It

It is ludicrous enough, that I began
to fear I should be betrothed to this
young lady; and when my master
asked me if I would stay there with her
behind him, as he was going away
with the ship, which had taken in the
tobacco again, I cried immediately,
and said I would not leave him. At
last, by stealth, one night I was sent on
board the ship again; and in a little
time we sailed for Guernsey, where she
was in part owned by a merchant, one
Nicholas Doberry. As I was now
amongst a people who had not their
faces scarred, like some of the African
nations where I had been, I was very
glad I did not let them ornament me
in that manner when I was with them.
When we arrived at Guernsey, my
master placed me to board and lodge
with one of his mates, who had a wife
and family there, and some months afterwards

wards he went to England, and left me in care of this mate, together, with my friend Dick: This mate had a little daughter, aged about five or six years, with whom I used to be much delighted. I had often obferved that when her mother washed her face it looked very rofy, but when-fhe washed mine it did not look fo: I therefore tried oftentimes myfelf if I could not by wafhing make my face of the fame colour as my little play-mate (Mary), but it was all in vain, and I now began to be mortified at the difference in our complexions. This woman behaved to me with great kindnefs and attention; and taught me every thing in the fame manner as fhe did her own child, and indeed in every refpect treated me as fuch. I remained here till the fummer of the year 1757; when my mafter, being appointed firft lieu-

tenant

tenant of his majesty's ship the Roebuck, sent for Dick and me, and
his old mate: on this we all left
Guernsey, and set out for England
in a sloop bound for London. As we
were coming up towards the Nore,
where the Roebuck lay, a man of war's
boat came alongside to press our people, on which each man ran to hide
himself. I was very much frightened
at this, though I did not know what it
meant, or what to think or do. However I went and hid myself also under a
hencoop. Immediately afterwards the
press-gang came on board with their
swords drawn, and searched all about,
pulled the people out by force, and put
them into the boat. At last I was found
out also; the man that found me held
me up by the heels while they all made
their sport of me, I roaring and crying
out all the time most lustily; but at
laft

laft the mate, who was my conductor, feeing this, came to my affiftance, and did all he could to pacify me, but all to very little purpofe, till I had feen the boat go off. Soon afterwards we came to the Nore, where the Roebuck lay; and, to our great joy, my mafter came on board to us, and brought us to the fhip. When I went on board this large fhip, I was amazed indeed to fee the quantity of men and the guns. However my furprife began to diminifh as my knowledge increafed; and I ceafed to feel thofe apprehenfions and alarms which had taken fuch ftrong poffeffion of me when I firft came among the Europeans, and for fome time after. I began now to pafs to an op- pofite extreme, I was fo far from being afraid of any thing new which I faw, that, after I had been fometime in this fhip, I even began to long for an engagement.

My

My griefs too, which in young minds are not perpetual, were now wearing away; and I soon enjoyed myself pretty well, and felt tolerably easy in my prefent fituation. There was a number of boys on board, which ftill made it more agreeable; for we were always together, and a great part of our time was fpent in play. I remained in this fhip a confiderable time, during which we made feveral cruifes, and vifited a variety of places: among others we were twice in Holland, and brought over feveral perfons of diftinction from it, whofe names I do not now remember. On the paffage, one day, for the diverfion of thofe gentlemen, all the boys were called on the quarter deck, and were paired proportionably, and then made to fight; after which the gentlemen gave the combatants from five to nine fhillings each. This was

the

rhe firſt time I ever fought with a white boy; and I nevei knew what it was to have a bloody noſe befoie. This made me fight moſt deſperately, I ſuppoſe conſiderably more than an hour: and at laſt, both of us being weary, we were parted. I had a great deal of this kind of ſport afteiwards, in which the captain and the ſhip's company uſed very much to encourage me. Sometime afterwards the ſhip went to Leith in Scotland, and from thence to the Orkneys, where I was ſurpriſed in ſeeing ſcarcely any night: and from thence we ſailed with a great fleet, full of ſoldiers, for England. All this time we had never come to an engagement, though we were frequently cruiſing off the coaſt of France: during which we chaſed many veſſels, and took in all ſeventeen prizes. I had been learning many of the manœuvres of the ſhip.

during

during our cruife; and I was feveral times made to fire the guns. One evening, off Havre de Grace, juft as it was growing dark, we were ftanding off fhore, and met with a fine large French-built frigate. We got all things immediately ready for fighting; and I now expected I fhould be gratified in feeing an engagement, which I had fo long wifhed for in vain. But the very moment the word of command was given to fire, we heard thofe on board the other fhip cry 'Haul down the jib;' and in that inftant fhe hoifted Englifh colours. There was inftantly with us an amazing cry of—'Avaft!' or ftop firing, and I think one or two guns had been let off, but happily they did no mifchief. We had hailed them feveral times, but they not hearing, we received no anfwer, which was the caufe of our firing. The boat was then fent

on

on board of her, and she proved to be
the Ambuscade man of war, to my no-
small disappointment. We returned to
Portsmouth, without having been in
any action, just at the trial of Admiral
Byng (whom I saw several times during it) and my master having left the
ship, and gone to London for promo-
tion, Dick and I were put on board the
Savage sloop of war, and we went in
her to assist in bringing off the St.
George man of war, that had ran ashore
somewhere on the coast. After staying
a few weeks on board the Savage, Dick
and I were sent on shore at Deal, where
we remained some short time, till my
master sent for us to London, the place
I had long desired exceedingly to see.
We therefore both with great pleasure
got into a waggon, and came to London, where we were received by a Mr.
Guerin, a relation of my master. This

gentleman

gentleman had two fifters, very amiable ladies, who took much notice and great care of me. Though I had defired fo much to fee London, when I arrived in it I was unfortunately unable to gratify my curiofity; for I had at this time the chilblains to fuch a degree that I could not ftand for feveral months, and I was obliged to be fent to St. George's Hofpital. There I grew fo ill, that the doctors wanted to cut my left leg off at different times, apprehending a mortification; but I always faid I would rather die than fuffer it; and happily (I thank God) I recovered without the operation. After being there feveral weeks, and juft as I had recovered, the fmall pox broke out on me, fo that I was again confined; and I thought myfelf now particularly unfortunate. However I foon recovered again; and by this time my

master

master having been promoted to be first
lieutenant of the Prefton man of war
of fifty guns, then new at Deptford,
D. k and I were fent on board her,
and foon after we went to Holland to
bring over the late Duke of ————
to England.—While I was in this fhip
an incident happened, which, though
trifling, I beg leave to relate, as I could
not help taking particular notice of it,
and confidering it then as a judgment of
God. One morning a young man was
looking up to the fore-top, and in a
wicked tone, common on fhipboard,
d—d his eyes about fomething. Juft
at the moment fome fmall particles
of dirt fell into his left eye, and by
the evening it was very much inflamed.
The next day it grew worfe, and within
fix or feven days he loft it. From
this fhip my mafter was appointed a
lieutenant on board the Royal George.
When

When he was going he wished me to
stay on board the Preston, to learn the
French horn; but the ship being ordered for Turkey I could not think of
leaving my master, to whom I was
very warmly attached, and I told him
if he left me behind it would break
my heart. This prevailed on him to
take me with him, but he left Dick on
board the Preston, whom I embraced
at parting for the last time. The Royal
George was the largest ship I had ever
seen; so that when I came on board of
her I was surprised at the number of
people, men, women, and children, of
every denomination; and the largeness
of the guns, many of them also of brass,
which I had never seen before. Here
were also shops or stalls of every kind
of goods, and people crying their different commodities about the ship as in
a town. To me it appeared a little
world,

3

world, into which I was again caft with
out a friend, for I had no longer my
dear companion Dick. We did not
ftay long here. My mafter was not
many weeks on board before he got an
appointment to be fixth lieutenant of
the Namur, which was then at Spithead, fitting up for Vice-admiral Bofcawen, who was going with a large fleet
on an expedition againft Louifburgh.
The crew of the Royal George were
turned over to her, and the flag of
that gallant admiral was hoifted on
board, the blue at the maintop gallant
maft head. There was a very great
fleet of men of war of every defcription affembled together for this expedition, and I was in hopes foon to have
an opportunity of being gratified with
a fea-fight. All things being now in
readinefs, this mighty fleet (for there
was alfo Admiral Cornifh's fleet in com-

pany,

pany, deftined for the Eaft Indies) at laft weighed anchor, and failed. The two fleets continued in company for feveral days, and then parted; Admiral Cornifh, in the Lenox, having firft fa‑luted our admiral in the Namur, which he returned. We then fteered for America; but, by contrary winds, we were driven to Teneriffe, where I was ftruck with its noted peak. Its prodi‑gious height, and its form, refembling a fugar loaf, filled me with wonder. We remained in fight of this ifland fome days, and then proceeded for America, which we foon made, and got into a very commodious harbour called St. George, in Halifax, where we had fifh in great plenty, and all other frefh provifions. We were here joined by different men of war and tranfport fhips with foldiers; after which, our fleet being increafed to a

prodigious

prodigious number of ships of all kinds, we failed for Cape Breton in Nova Scotia. We had the good and gallant General Wolfe on board our ship, whose affability made him highly esteemed and beloved by all the men. He often honoured me, as well as other boys, with marks of his notice; and saved me once a flogging for fighting with a young gentleman. We arrived at Cape Breton in the summer of 1758: and here the soldiers were to be landed, in order to make an attack upon Louisbourgh. My master had some part in superintending the landing, and here I was in a small measure gratified in seeing an encounter between our men and the enemy. The French were posted on the shore to receive us, and disputed our landing for a long time; but at last they were driven from their trenches, and a complete landing was effected. Our troops purfued them as far as the town of Louifbourgh. In this action many were killed on both fides. One thing remarkable I faw this day —A lieutenant of the Princefs Amelia, ho, as well as my mafter, fuperintended a landing, was giving the word of command, and while his mouth was oper a mufquet ball went through it, and paffed out at his cheek. I had that day in my hand the fcalp of an indian king, who was killed in the engagement: the fcalp had been taken off by an Highlander. I faw this king's ornaments too, which were very curious, and made of feathers.

Our land forces laid fiege to the town of Louifbourgh, while the French men of war were blocked up in the harbour by the fleet, the batteries at the fame time playing upon them from the land. This they did with fuch effect, that one

day

day I faw fome of the fhips fet on fire by the fhells from the batteries, and I believe two or three of them were quite burnt. At another time, about fifty boats belonging to the Englifh men of war, commanded by Captain George Belfour of the Ætna fire fhip, and Mr. Laforey another junior captain, attacked and boarded the only two remaining French men of war in the harbour. They alfo fet fire to a feventy-gun fhip, but a fixty-four, called the Bienfaifant, they brought off. During my ftay here I had often an opportunity of being near captain Belfour, who was pleafed to notice me, and liked me fo much that he often afked my mafter to let him have me, but he would not part with me, and no confideration could have induced me to leave him. At laft Louifbourgh was taken, and the Englifh men of war came into the harbour

before

before it, to my very great joy; for I had now more liberty of indulging myself, and I went often on shore. When the ships were in the harbour we had the most beautiful procession on the water I ever saw. All the admirals and captains of the men of war, full dressed, and in their barges, well ornamented with pendants, came alongside of the Namur. The vice-admiral then went on shore in his barge, followed by the other officers in order of seniority, to take possession, as I suppose, of the town and fort. Some time after this the French governor and his lady, and other persons of note, came on board our ship to dine. On this occasion our ships were dressed with colours of all kinds, from the topgallant-mast head to the deck, and this, with the firing of guns, formed a most grand and magnificent spectacle.

As

As foon as every thing here was
fettled, Admiral Bofcawen failed with
part of the fleet for England, leaving
fome fhips behind with Rear admirals
Sir Charles Hardy and Durell. It was
now winter, and one evening, during
our paffage home, about dufk, when
we were in the channel, or near found-
ings, and were beginning to look for
land, we defcried feven fail of large
men of war, which ftood off fhore.
Several people on board of our fhip
faid, as the two fleets were (in forty
minutes from the firft fight) within hail
of each other, that they were Englifh
men of war, and fome of our people
even began to name fome of the fhips.
By this time both fleets began to min-
gle, and our admiral ordered his flag
to be hoifted. At that inftant the other
fleet, which were French, hoifted their
enfigns, and gave us a broadfide as they

G 3   paffed

paffed by. Nothing could create greater
furprife and confufion among us than
this. the wind was high, the fea rough,
and we had our lower and middle deck
guns noufed in, fo that not a fingle gun
on board was ready te be fired at any
of the French fhips. However, the
Royal William and the Somerfet, being
our fternmoft fhips, became a little prepared, and each gave the French fhips a
broadfide as they paffed by. I afterwards heard this was a French fqua-
dron, commanded by Monf. Conflans;
and certainly had the Frenchmen known
our condition, and had a mind to fight
us, they might have done us great
mifchief. But we were not long before
we were prepared for an engagement.
Immediately many things were toffed
overboard; the fhips were made ready
for fighting as foon as poffible; and
about ten at night we had bent a new

main-

main fail, the old one being fplit. Being now in readinefs for fighting, we wore fhip, and ftood after the French fleet, who were one or two fhips in number more than we. However we gave them chafe, and continued purfuing them all night; and at day-light we faw fix of them, all large fhips of the line, and an Englifh Eaft Indiaman, a prize they had taken. We chafed them all day till between three and four o'clock in the evening, when we came up with, and paffed within a mufquet fhot of one feventy-four gun fhip, and the Indiaman alfo, who now hoifted her colours, but immediately hauled them down again. On this we made a fignal for the other fhips to take poffeffion of her; and, fuppofing the man of war would likewife ftrike, we cheered, but fhe did not; though if we had fired into her, from being fo near, we muft have taken her. To my utter furprife,

the

the Somerset, who was the next ship a-stern of the Namur, made way likewife, and, thinking they were fure of this French ship, they cheered in the fame manner, but still continued to follow us. The French Commodore was about a gun-shot ahead of all, running from us with all speed, and about four o'clock he carried his foretopmast overboard. This caufed another loud cheer with us; and a little after the topmast came clofe by us, but, to our great furprife, inftead of coming up with her, we found fhe went as faft as ever, if not fafter. The fea grew now much fmoother; and the wind lulling, the feventy-four gun ship we had paffed came again by us in the very fame direction, and fo near, that we heard her people talk as fhe went by; yet not a fhot was fired on either fide; and about five or fix o'clock, juft as it grew dark, fhe joined her commodore.

commodore. We chafed all night;
but the next day we were out of fight,
fo that we faw no more of them;
and we only had the old Indiaman
(called Carnarvon I think) for our
trouble. After this we ftood in for
the channel, and foon made the land;
and, about the clofe of the year
1758—9, we got fafe to St. Helen's.
Here the Namur ran aground, and
alfo another large fhip aftern of us;
but, by ftarting our water, and toffing
many things overboud to lighten
her, we got the fhips off without
any damage. We ftayed for a fhort
time at Spithead, and then went into
Portfmouth harbour to refit. from
whence the admiral went to London,
and my mafter and I foon followed,
with a prefs-gang, as we wanted fome
hands to complete our complement.

G 5   CHAP.

C H A P. IV.

The author is baptized—Narrowly escapes drowning—Goes on an expedition to the Mediterranean—Incidents he met with there—Is witness to an engagement between some English and French ships—A particular account of the celebrated engagement between Admiral Boscawen and Monf. Le Clue, off Cape Logos, in August 1759—Dreadful explosion of a French ship—The author sails for England—His master appointed to the command of a fire-ship—Meets a negro boy, from whom he experiences much benevolence—Prepares for an expedition against Belle-Isle—A remarkable story of a disaster which befel his ship—Arrives at Belle-Isle—Operations of the landing and

*and siege—The author's danger and dif-
tress, with his manner of extricating
himself—Surrender of Belle-Isle—Tranfactions afterwards on the coast of France
—Remarkable instance of kidnapping—
The author returns to England—Hears
a talk of peace, and expects his freedom—
His ship sails for Deptford to be paid
off, and when he arrives there he is
suddenly seized by his master and carried
forcibly on board a West India ship and
sold.*

IT was now between two and three
years since I first came to England, a
great part of which I had spent at sea;
so that I became inured to that service,
and began to consider myself as happily
situated, for my master treated me always extremely well, and my attach-
ment and gratitude to him were very
great. From the various scenes I had

G 6   beheld

beheld on ſhip-board, I ſoon grew a ſtranger to terror of every kind, and was, in that reſpect at leaſt, almoſt an Engliſhman. I have often reflected with ſurpriſe that I never felt half the alarm at any of the numerous dangers I have been in, that I was filled with at the firſt ſight of the Europeans, and at every act of theirs, even the moſt trifling, when I firſt came among them, and for ſome time afterwards. That fear, however, which was the effect of my ignorance, wore away as I began to know them. I could now ſpeak Engliſh tolerably well, and I perfectly underſtood every thing that was ſaid. I not only felt myſelf quite eaſy with theſe new countrymen, but reliſhed their ſociety and manners. I no longer looked upon them as ſpirits, but as men ſuperior to us ; and there-fore I had the ſtronger deſire to re-

ſemble

femble them; to imbibe their fpirit, and imitate their manners. I therefore embraced every occafion of improvement; and every new thing that I obferved I treafured up in my memory. I had long wifhed to be able to read and write, and for this purpofe I took every opportunity to gain inftruction, but had made as yet very little progrefs. However, when I went to London with my mafter, I had foon an opportunity of improving myfelf, which I gladly embraced. Shortly after my arrival, he fent me to wait upon the Mifs Guerins, who had treated me with much kindnefs when I was there before; and they fent me to fchool.

While I was attending thefe ladies, their fervants told me I could not go to Heaven, unlefs I was baptized. This made me very uneafy, for I had now fome faint idea of a future ftate.

accordingly

accordingly I communicated my anxiety to the eldeft Mifs Guerin, with whom I was become a favourite, and preffed her to have me baptized; when to my great joy, fhe told me I fhould. She had formerly afked my mafter to let me be baptized, but he had refufed; however fhe now infifted on it; and he being under fome obligation to her brother complied with her requeft; fo I was baptized in St. Margaret's church, Weftminfter, in February 1759, by my prefent name. The clergyman at the fame time, gave me a book, called a Guide to the Indians, written by the Bifhop of Sodor and Man. On this occafion, Mifs Guerin did me the honour to ftand as godmother, and afterwards gave me a treat. I ufed to attend thefe ladies about the town, in which fervice I was extremely happy; as I had thus many opportunities of

feeing

feeing London, which I defired of all things. 1 was fometimes, however, with my mafter at his rendezvous-houfe, which was at the foot of Weft-minfter-bridge. Here I ufed to enjoy myfelf in playing about the bridge ftairs, and often in the watermen's wherries, with other boys. On one of thefe occafions there was another boy with me in a wherry, and we went out into the current of the river: while we were there, two more ftout boys came to us in another wherry, and, abufing us for taking the boat, defired me to get into the other wherry-boat. Accord-ingly I went to get out of the wherry I was in, but juft as I had got one of my feet into the other boat, the boys fhoved it off, fo that I fell into the Thames; and, not being able to fwim, I fhould unavoidably have been drowned, but for the affiftance of fome

watermen

watermen who providentially came to my relief.

The Namur being again got ready for sea, my master, with his gang, was ordered on board; and, to my no small grief, I was obliged to leave my school-master, whom I liked very much, and always attended while I stayed in London, to repair on board with my master. Nor did I leave my kind pa-troneffes, the Mifs Guerins, without uneafinefs and regret. They often ufed to teach me to read, and took great pains to inftruct me in the prin-ciples of religion and the knowledge of God. I therefore parted from thofe amiable ladies with reluctance · after receiving from them many friendly cautions how to conduct myfelf, and fome valuable prefents.

When I came to Spithead, I found we were deftined for the Mediterra-nean,

nean, with a large fleet, which was now ready to put to sea. We only waited for the arrival of the admiral, who soon came on board; and about the beginning of the spring 1759, having weighed anchor, and got under way, sailed for the Mediterranean; and in eleven days, from the Land's End, we got to Gibraltar. While we were here I used to be often on shore, and got various fruits in great plenty, and very cheap.

I had frequently told several people, in my excursions on shore, the story of my being kidnapped with my sister, and of our being separated, as I have related before; and I had as often expressed my anxiety for her fate, and my sorrow at having never met her again. One day, when I was on shore, and mentioning these circumstances to some persons, one of them told me he knew

where

where my fister was, and, if I would accompany him, he would bring me to her. Improbable as this story was, I believed it immediately, and agreed to go with him, while my heart leaped for joy; and, indeed, he conducted me to a black young woman, who was so like my fister, that at first fight, I really thought it was her: but I was quickly undeceived; and, on talking to her, I found her to be of another nation.

While we lay here the Prefton came in from the Levant. As foon as fhe arrived, my mafter told me I fhould now fee my old companion, Dick, who was gone in her when fhe failed for Turkey. I was much rejoiced at this news, and expected every minute to embrace him, and when the captain came on board of our fhip, which he did immediately after, I ran to inquire after my friend; but, with inexpreffible

neffible forrow, I learned from the boat's crew that the dear youth was dead! and that they had brought his cheft, and all his other things, to my mafter; thefe he afterwards gave to me, and I regarded them as a memorial of my friend, whom I loved, and grieved for, as a brother.

While we were at Gibralter, I faw a foldier hanging by the heels, at one of the moles*: I thought this a ftrange fight, as I had feen a man hanged in London by his neck. At another time I faw the mafter of a frigate towed to fhore on a grating, by feveral of the men of war's boats, and difcharged the fleet, which I underftood was a mark of difgrace for cowardice. On board the fame fhip there was alfo a failor hung up at the yard-arm.

After lying at Gibralter for fome

*He had drowned himfelf in endeavouring to defert.

time,

time, we failed up the Mediterranean a confiderable way above the Gulf of Lyons; where we were one night overtaken with a terrible gale of wind, much greater than any I had ever yet experienced. The fea ran fo high that, though all the guns were well houfed, there was great reafon to fear their getting loofe, the fhip rolled fo much; and if they had it muft have proved our deftruction. After we had cruifed here for a fhort time, we came to Barcelona, a Spanifh fea-port, remarkable for its filk manufactures. Here the fhips were all to be watered; and my mafter, who fpoke different languages, and ufed often to interpret for the admiral, fuperintended the watering of ours. For that purpofe he and the officers of the other fhips, who were on the fame fervice, had tents pitched in the bav; and the Spanifh foldiers were ftationed along the fhore, I fup-

pofe

pofe to fee that no depredations were committed by our men.

I ufed conftantly to attend my master; and I was charmed with this place. All the time we ftayed it was like a fair with the natives, who brought us fruits of all kinds, and fold them to us much cheaper than I got them in England. They ufed alfo to bring wine down to us in hog and fheep fkins, which diverted me very much. The Spanifh officers here treated our officers with great politenefs and attention; and fome of them, in particular, ufed to come often to my mafter's tent to vifit him; where they would fometimes divert themfelves by mounting me on the horfes or mules, fo that I could not fall, and fetting them off at full gallop; my imperfect fkill in horfemanfhip all the while affording them no fmall entertainment. After the fhips were

watered,

watered, we returned to our old ſta-
tion of cruizing off Toulon, for the
purpoſe of intercepting a fleet of French
men of war that lay there. One Sunday, in our cruiſe, we came off a place
where there were two ſmall French frigates lying in ſhore; and our admiral,
thinking to take or deſtroy them, ſent
two ſhips in after them—the Culloden
and the Conqueror. They ſoon came
up to the Frenchmen; and I ſaw a
ſmart fight here, both by ſea and land:
for the frigates were covered by batteries, and they played upon our ſhips
moſt furiouſly, which they as furiouſly
returned, and for a long time a conſtant firing was kept up on all ſides at
an amazing rate. At laſt one frigate
ſunk; but the people eſcaped, though
not without much difficulty · and a
little after ſome of the people left the
other frigate alſo, which was a mere
wreck.

wreck. However, our ſhips did not venture to bring her away, they were ſo much annoyed from the batteries, which raked them both in going and coming: their topmaſts were ſhot a-way, and they were otherwiſe ſo much ſhattered, that the admiral was obliged to ſend in many boats to tow them back to the fleet. I afterwards ſailed with a man who fought in one of the French batteries during the engage-ment, and he told me our ſhips had done conſiderable miſchief that day on ſhore and in the batteries.

After this we ſailed for Gibraltar, and arrived there about Auguſt 1759. Here we remained with all our ſails un-bent, while the fleet was watering and doing other neceſſary things. While we were in this ſituation, one day the admiral, with moſt of the principal of-ficers, and many people of all ſtations, being

being on fhore, about feven o'clock
in the evening we were alarmed by
fignals from the frigates ftationed for
that purpofe; and in an inftant there
was a general cry that the French fleet
was out, and juft paffing through the
ftreights. The admiral immediately
came on board with fome other officers, and it is impoffible to defcribe
the noife, hurry and confufion throughout the whole ficet, in bending their
fails and flipping their cables; many
people and fhips' boats were left on
fhore in the buftle. We had two
captains on board of our fhip who came
away in the hurry and left their fhips
to follow. We fhewed lights from the
gun-wales to the main top maft-head;
and all our lieutenants were employed
amongft the fleet to tell the fhips not
to wait for ther captains, but to put
the fails to the yards, flip their cables

and

and follow us; and in this confusion of making ready for fighting, we set out for sea in the dark after the French fleet. Here I could have exclaimed with Ajax,

"Oh Jove! O father! if it be thy will
"That we must perish, we thy will obey,
"But let us perish by the light of day.'

They had got the start of us so far that we were not able to come up with them during the night; but at day-light we saw seven sail of the line of bat l some miles ahead. We immediately chased them till about four o'clock in the evening, when our ships came up with them, and, though we were about fifteen large ships, our gall nt admiral only fought them with his own division, which consisted of seven; so that we were just ship for ship. We passed by the whole of the enemy's fleet in order to come at their commander, Monf. La Clue, who was in the Ocean, an eighty-four gun fhip as we pafsed they all fired on us, and at one time three of them fired together, continuing to do fo for fome time. Notwithftanding which our admiral would not fuffer a gun to be fired at any of them, to my aftonifhment; but made us lie on our bellies on the deck till we came quite clofe to the Ocean, who was ahead of them all, when we had orders to pour the whole three tiers into her at once.

The engagement now commenced with great fury on both fides the Ocean immediately returned our fire, and we continued engaged with each other for fome time; during which I was frequently ftunned with the thundering of the great guns, whofe dreadful contents hurried many of my companions into awful eternity. At laft the French

line

line was entirely broken, and we obtained the victory, which was immediately proclaimed with loud huzzas and acclamations. We took three prizes, La Modeſte, of ſixty-four guns, and Le Temeraire and Centaur, of seventy-four guns each. The reſt of the French ſhips took to flight with all the ſail they could crowd. Our ſhip being very much damaged, and quite diſabled from purſuing the enemy, the admiral immediately quitted her, and went in the broken and only boat we had left on board the Newark, with which, and ſome other ſhips, he went after the French. The Ocean, and another large French ſhip, called the Redoubtable, endeavouring to eſcape, ran aſhore at Cape Logas, on the coaſt of Portugal; and the French admiral and ſome of the crew got aſhore; but we, finding it impoſſible to get the ſhips

off,

oil, set fire to them both. About midnight I saw the Ocean blow up, with a moft dreadful explofion. I never beheld a more awful fcene. In lefs than a minute, the midnight for a certain fpace feemed turned into day by the blaze, which was attended with a noife louder and more terrible than thunder, that feemed to rend even element around us.

My ftation during the engagement was on the middle-deck, where I was quartered with another boy, to bring powder to the aftermoft gun; and here I was a witnefs of the dreadful fate of many of my companions, who, in the twinkling of an eye, were dafhed in pieces, and launched into eternity. Happily I efcaped unhurt, though the fhot and fplinters flew thick about me during the whole fight. Towards the latter part of it my mafter was wound-

2   ed,

ed, and I saw him carried down to the furgeon, but though I was much alarmed for him and wished to assist him I dared not leave my post. At this station my gun-mate (a partner in bringing powder for the same gun) and I ran a very great risk for more than half an hour of blowing up the ship. For, when we had taken the cartridges out of the boxes, the bottoms of many of them proving rotten, the powder ran all about the deck, near the match tub. we scarcely had water enough at the last to throw on it. We were also, from our employment, very much exposed to the enemy's shots, for we had to go through nearly the whole length of the ship to bring the powder. I expected therefore every minute to be my last, especially when I saw our men fall so thick about me; but, wishing to guard as much against

the

the dangers as poſſible, at firſt I thought
it would be ſafeſt not to go for the
p ler till the Frenchmen had fired
th roadſide, and then, while they
we gging, I could go and come
w.t powder but immediately after-
ward though this caution was fruit-
leſs, d, cerning nv'd with the re-
fectio that there was a time allotted
for n o die as well as to be born, I
inſtan caſt off all fear or thought
whatev of death, and went through
the w le of my duty with alacrity,
pleaſing myſelf with the hope, if I ſur-
vived the battle, of relating it and the
danger I had eſcaped to the Miſs
Guerin, and others, when I ſhould return to London.

Our ſhip ſuffered very much in this
engagement, for, beſides the number
of our killed and wounded, ſhe was almoſt torn to pieces, and our rigging ſo
much

much shattered, that our mizen-mast, main-yard, &c. hung over the side of the ship, so that we were obliged to get many carpenters, and others from some of the ships of the fleet, to assist in setting us in some tolerable order, and, notwithstanding which, it took us some time before we were completely refitted, after which we left Admiral Broderick to command, and we, with the prizes steered for England. On the passage, and as soon as my master was something recovered of his wounds, the admiral appointed him captain of the Ætna fire-ship, on which he and I left the Namur, and went on board of her at sea. I liked this little ship very much. I now became the captain's steward, in which situation I was very happy: for I was extremely well treated by all on board, and I had leisure to improve myself in

H 4   reading

... ... The latter of these
I formed a little on before I left the Na-
my, as there was a school on board.
When we arrived at Spithead, the
Ætna went into Portsmouth harbour
to refit, which being done, we returned
to Spithead and joined a large fleet that
was thought to be intended against the
Havannah, but about that time the
king died, whether that prevented the
expedition I know not; but it caused
our ship to be stationed at Cowes, in
the isle of Wight, till the beginning of
the year sixty-one. Here I spent my
time very pleasantly, I was much on
shore all about this delightful island,
and found the inhabitants very civil.

'While I was here, I met with a
trifling incident, which surprised me
agreeably. I was one day in a field
belonging to a gentleman who had a
black boy about my own size, this boy
having

having obferved me from his mafter's houfe, was tranfported at the fight of one of his own countrymen, and ran to meet me with the utmoft hafte. I not knowing what he was about, turned a little out of his way at firft, but to no purpofe he foon came clofe to me and caught hold of me in his arms as if I had been his brother, though we had never feen each other before. After we had talked together for fome time he took me to his mafter's houfe, where I was treated very kindly. This benevolent boy and I were very happy in frequently feeing each other till about the month of March 1761, when our fhip had orders to fit out again for another expedition. When we got ready, we joined a very large fleet at Spithead, commanded by Commodore Keppel, which was deftined againft Bele-Ifle, and with a number of tranf-

H 5

port ships with troops on board to make a defcent on the place, we failed once more in queft of fame. I longed to engage in new adventures and fee frefh wonders.

I had a mind on which every thing uncommon made its full impreffion, and every event which I confidered as marvellous. Every extraordinary efcape, or fignal deliverance, either of myfelf or others, I looked upon to be effected by the interpofition of Providence. We had not been above ten days at fea before an incident of this kind happened; which, whatever credit it may obtain from the reader, made no fmall impreffion on my mind

We had on board a gunner, whofe name was John Mondle; a man of very indifferent morals. This man's cabin was between the decks, exactly over where I lay, abreaft of the quarter-deck ladder.

ladder. One night, the 5th of April, being terrified with a dream, he awoke in so great a fright that he could not rest in his bed any longer, nor even remain in his cabin, and he went upon deck about four o'clock in the morning extremely agitated. He immediately told those on the deck of the agonies of his mind, and the dream which occasioned it; in which he said he had seen many things very awful, and had been warned by St. Peter to repent, who told him time was short. This he said had greatly alarmed him, and he was determined to alter his life. People generally mock the fears of others when they are themselves in safety, and some of his shipmates who heard him only laughed at him. However, he made a vow that he never would drink strong liquors again, and he immediately got a light, and gave away his sea-stores

of

of liquor. After which, his agitation ftill continuing, he began to read the Scriptures, hoping to find fome relief, and foon afterwards he laid himfelf down again on his bed, and endeavoured to compofe himfelf to fleep, but to no purpofe, his mind ftill continuing in a ftate of agony. By this time it was exactly half after feven in the morning I was then under the half-deck at the great cabin door; and all at once I heard the people in the waift cry out moft fearfully—'The Lord have mercy ' upon us' We are all loft' The ' Lord have mercy upon us!' Mr. Mondle hearing the cries, immediately ran out of his cabin, and we were inftantly ftruck by the Lynne, a forty-gun fhip, Captain Clark, which nearly ran us down. This fhip had juft put about, and was by the wind, but had not got full headway, or we muft all

have

have perished, for the wind was brisk. However, before Mr Mondle had got four steps from his cabin door, she struck our ship with her cutwater right in the middle of his bed and cabin, and ran it up to the combings of the quarter deck hatchway, and above three feet below water, and in a minute there was not a bit of wood to be seen where Mr. Mondle's cabin stood; and he was so near being killed that some of the splinters tore his face. As Mr. Mondle must inevitably have perished from this accident had he not been alarmed in the very extraordinary way I have related, I could not help regarding this as an awful interposition of Providence for his preservation. The two ships for some time swinged alongside of each other; for ours being a fireship, our grappling-irons caught the Lynne every way, and the yards and rigging went at an aftonifhing rate. Our fhip was in fuch a fhocking condition that we all thought fhe would inftantly go down, and every one ran for their lives, and got as well as they could on board the Lynne; but our lieutenant being the aggreffor, he never quitted the fhip. However, when we found fhe did not fink immediately, the captain came on board again, and encouraged our people to return and try to fave her. Many on this came back, but fome would not venture. Some of the fhips in the fleet, feeing our fituation, immediately fent their boats to our affiftance; but it took us the whole day to fave the fhip with all their help. And by ufing every poffible means, particularly frapping her together with many hawfers, and putting a great quantity of tallow below water where fhe was damaged, fhe was kept to-gether:

gether: but it was well we did not meet with any gales of wind, or we muft have gone to pieces, for we were in fuch a crazy condition that we had fhips to attend us till we arrived at Belle-Ifle, the place of our deftination; and then we had all things taken out of the fhip, and fhe was propeily repaired. This efcape of Mr. Mondle, which he, as well as myfelf, always confidered as a fingular act of Providence, I believe had a great influence on his life and conduct ever afterwards.

Now that I am on this fubject I beg leave to relate another inftance or two which ftrongly raifed my belief of the particular interpofition of Heaven, and which might not otherways have found a place here, from their infignificance. I belonged for a few days in the year 1758, to the Jafon, of fifty-four guns, at Plymouth; and one night, when I

was

was on board, a woman, with a child at her breaft, fell from the upper-deck down into the hold, near the keel Every one thought that the mother and child muft be both dafhed to pieces, but, to our great furprife, neither of them was hurt I myfelf one day fell headlong from the upper-deck of the Ætna down the after-hold, when the ballaft was out, and all who faw me fall cried out I was killed. but I received not the leaft injury. And in the fame fhip a man fell from the maft-head on the deck without being hurt In thefe, and in many more inftances, I thought I could plainly trace the hand of God, without whofe permif-fion a fparrow cannot fall. I began to raife my fear from man to him alone, and to call daily on his holy name with fear and reverence. and I truft he heard my fupplications, and gracioufly

condefcended

condescended to answer me according to his holy word, and to implant the feeds of piety in me, even one of the meanest of his creatures.

When we had refitted our ship, and all things were in readiness for attacking the place, the troops on board the transports were ordered to disembark; and my master as a junior captain, had a share in the command of the landing. This was on the 12th of April. The French were drawn up on the shore, and had made every difposition to oppofe the landing of our men, only a fmall part of them this day being able to effect it, moft of them, after fighting with great bravery, were cut off, and General Crawford, with a number of others, were taken prifoners. In this day's engagement we had also our lieutenant killed.

On the 21ft of April we renewed our efforts

efforts to land the men, while all the men of war were stationed along the shore to cover it, and fired at the French batteries and breastworks from early in the morning till about four o'clock in the evening, when our soldiers effected a safe landing. They immediately attacked the French; and, after a sharp encounter, forced them from the batteries. Before the enemy retreated they blew up several of them, left they should fall into our hands. Our men now proceeded to besiege the citadel, and my master was ordered on shore to superintend the landing of all the materials necessary for carrying on the siege, in which service I mostly attended him. While I was there I went about to different parts of the island; and one day, particularly, my curiosity almost cost me my life. I wanted very much to see the mode of charging the

mortar,

mortars and letting off the shells, and for that purpose I went to an English battery that was but a very few yards from the walls of the citadel. There, indeed, I had an opportunity of completely gratifying myself in seeing the whole operation, and that not without running a very great risk, both from the English shells that burst while I was there, but likewise from those of the French. One of the largest of their shells bursted within nine or ten yards of me there was a single rock close by, about the size of a butt; and I got instant shelter under it in time to avoid the fury of the shell. Where it burst the earth was torn in such a manner that two or three butts might easily have gone into the hole it made, and it threw great quantities of stones and dirt to a considerable distance. Three shot were also fired at me and another

boy

boy who was along with me, one of
them in particular seemed

" Wing'd with re ' lightning and impetuous rage, '

for with a moft dreadful found it hiffed
clofe by me, and ftruck a rock at a
little diftance, which it fhattered to
pieces. When I faw what perilous
circumftances I was in, I attempted
to return the neareft way I could find,
and thereby I got between the Englifh
and the French centinels. An Englifh
ferjeant, who commanded the outpofts,
feeing me, and furprifed how I came
there, (which was by ftealth along the
feafhore), reprimanded me very feverely
for it, and inftantly took the centinel
off his poft into cuftody, for his negligence in fuffering me to pafs the
lines. While I was in this fituation
I obferved at a little diftance a French
horfe, belonging to fome iflanders,
which I thought I would now mount,

for the greater expedition of getting off
Accordingly I took fome cord which I
had about me, and making a kind of
bridle of it, I put it round the horfe's
head, and the tame beaft very quietly
fuffered me to tie him thus and mount
him. As foon as I was on the horfe's
back I began to kick and beat him, and
try every means to make him go quick,
but all to very little purpofe I could not
drive him out of a flow pace. While
I was creeping along, ftill within reach
of the enemy's fhot, I met with a fer-
vant well mounted on an Englifh horfe,
I immediately ftopped; and, crying,
told him my cafe, and begged of him
to help me, and this he effectually did;
for, having a fine large whip, he began to lafh my horfe with it fo feverely, that he fet off full fpeed with
me towards the fea, while I was quite
unable to hold or manage him. In
this

this manner I went along till I came to a craggy precipice. I now could not stop my horse, and my mind was filled with apprehensions of my deplorable fate should he go down the precipice, which he appeared fully disposed to do. I therefore thought I had better throw myself off him at once, which I did immediately with a great deal of dexterity, and fortunately escaped unhurt. As foon as I found myself at liberty I made the best of my way for the ship, determined I would not be so fool-hardy again in a hurry.

We continued to besiege the citadel till June, when it surrendered. During the siege I have counted above sixty shells and carcases in the air at once. When this place was taken I went through the citadel, and in the bomb-proofs under it, which were cut in the solid rock, and I thought it a surprising place,

place, both for ftrength and building. notwithftanding which our fhots and fhells had made amazing devaftation, and ruinous heaps all around it.

After the taking of this ifland, our fhips with fome others commanded by commodore Stanhope in the Swift-fure, went to Baffe-road, where we blocked up a French fleet. Our fhips were there from June till February following; and in that time I faw a great many fcenes of war, and ftratagems on both fides to deftroy each others fleet. Sometimes we would attack the French with fome fhips of the line, at other times with boats; and frequently we made prizes. Once or twice the French attacked us by throwing fhells with their bomb-veffels, and one day as a French veffel was throwing fhells at our fhips fhe broke from her fprings, behind the ifle of I de Re. the tide be-

3

ing

ing complicated, she came within a gun
shot of the Naffau, but the Naffau could
not bring a gun to bear upon her,
and thereby the Frenchman got off.
We were twice attacked by their fire
floats, which they chained together,
and then let them float down with the
tide, but each time we fent boats with
graplings, and towed them fafe out of
the fleet.

We had different commanders while
we were at this place, Commodores
Stanhope, Dennis, Lord Howe, &c
From hence, before the Spanish war
began, our ship and the Wafp floop
were fent to St. Sebaftian in Spain, by
Commodore Stanhope, and Commodore Dennis afterwards fent our ship as
a cartel to Bayonne in France*, after
which

*Among others whom we brought from Bayonne,
were two gentlemen, who had been in the West
Indie,

which † we went in February in 1762, to Belle-Ifle, and there ftaid till the fummer, when we left it, and returned to Portfmouth.

After our fhip was fitted out again for fervice, in September fhe went to Guernfey, where I was very glad to fee

Indies, where they fold flaves, and they confeffed they had made at one time a falfe bill of fale,
and fold two Portuguefe white men among a lot
of flaves.

᷄m people have it, that fometimes fhortly
before perfons die, their ward has been feen that
is, fome fpirit exactly in their likenefs, though
they are themfelves at other places at the fame
time One day while we were at Bayorne, Mr.
Mondle faw one of our men, as he thought, in the
gun room, and a little after, coming on the quarter deck, he fpoke of fome circumftances of this
man to fome of the officers They told him that
the man was then out of the fhip, in one of the
boats with the Lieutenant but Mr. Mondle
could not believe it, and we fearched the fhip,
when he found the man was actually out of her;
and when the boat returned fome time afterwards,
we found the man had been crowned the
very time Mr. Mondle thought he faw him

my old hostess, who was now a widow, and my former little charming companion, her daughter. I spent some time here very happily with them, till October, when we had orders to repair to Portsmouth. We parted from each other with a great deal of affection, and I promised to return soon, and see them again; not knowing what all-powerful fate had determined for me. Our ship having arrived at Portsmouth, we went into the harbour, and remained there till the latter end of November, when we heard great talk about a peace, and, to our very great joy, in the beginning of December we had orders to go up to London with our ship to be paid off. We received this news with loud huzzas, and every other demonstration of gladness; and nothing but mirth was to be seen throughout every part of the ship.

ship I too was not without my
share of the general joy on this occasion. I thought now of nothing but
being freed, and working for myself,
and thereby getting money to enable
me to get a good education; for I always had a great desire to be able at
least to read and write; and while I
was on ship-board I had endeavoured
to improve myself in both. While I
was in the Ætna particularly, the captain's clerk taught me to write, and
gave me a smattering of arithmetic
as far as the rule of three. There was
also one Daniel Queen, about forty
years of age, a man very well educat-
ed, who messed with me on board this
ship, and he likewise dressed and attended the captain. Fortunately this
man soon became very much attached
to me, and took very great pains to instruct me in many things. He taught

me

me to shave and dress hair a little, and also to read in the Bible, explaining many passages to me, which I did not comprehend. I was wonderfully surprised to see the laws and rules of my own country written almost exactly here, a circumstance which I believe tended to imprise our manners and customs more deeply on my memory. I used to tell him of this resemblance, and many a time we have sat up the whole night together at this employment. In short, he was like a father to me, and some even used to call me after his name, they also styled me the black Christian. Indeed I almost loved him with the affection of a son. Many things I have denied myself that he might have them, and when I used to play at marbles or any other game, and won a few halfpence, or got any little money, which I some-

times

times did, for shaving a man, I used
to buy him a little sugar or tobacco,
as far as my stock of money would go.
He used to say, that he and I never
should part, and that when our ship
was paid off, as I was as free as himself or any other man on board, he
would instruct me in his business, by
which I might gain a good livelihood.
This gave me new life and spirits, and
my heart burned within me, while I
thought the time long till I obtained
my freedom. For though my master
had not promised it to me, yet, besides
the assurances I had received that he
had no right to detain me, he always
treated me with the greatest kindness,
and reposed in me an unbounded con-
fidence ; he even paid attention to my
morals, and would never suffer me to
deceive him, or tell lies, of which he
used to tell me the consequences ; and

I 3   that

that if I did so God would not love me, so that from all this tendency, I had never once supposed, in all my dreams of freedom, that he would think of detaining me any longer than I pleased.

In pursuance of our orders we failed from Portsmouth for the Thames, and arrived at Deptford the 10th of December, where we cast anchor just as it was high water. The ship was up about half an hour, when my master ordered the barge to be manned, and all in an instant, without having before given me the least reason to suspect any thing of the matter, he forced me into the barge; saying, I was going to leave him, but he would take care I should not. I was so struck with the unexpectedness of this proceeding, that for some time I did not make a reply, only I made an offer to go for my

books

books and chest of clothes, but he
swore I should not move out of his
sight, and if I did he would cut my
throat, at the same time taking his
hanger. I began, however, to collect
myself, and, plucking up courage,
I told him I was free, and he could
not by law serve me so. But this only
enraged him the more, and he continued to swear, and said he would
soon let me know whether he would or
not, and at that instant sprung himself into the barge from the ship, to
the astonishment and sorrow of all on
board. The tide, rather unluckily for
me, had just turned downward, so that
we quickly fell down the river along
with it, till we came among some out-
ward-bound West Indiamen, for he
was resolved to put me on board the
first vessel he could get to receive me.
The boat's crew, who pulled against

I 4   their

then all, became quite faint different times, and would have gone ashore, but he would not let them. Some of them strove then to cheer me, and told me he could not sell me, and that they would stand by me, which revived me a little; and I still entertained hopes, for as they pulled along he asked some vessels to receive me, but they would not. But, just as we had got a little below Gravesend, we came alongside of a ship which was going away the next tide for the West Indies, her name was the Charming Sally, Captain James Doran, and my master went on board and agreed with him for me; and in a little time I was sent for into the cabin. When I came there Captain Doran asked me if I knew him: I answered that I did not, ‘Then,’ said he, ‘you are now my slave.’ I told him my master could not sell me

to

to him, nor to any one elfe 'Why,' faid
he, ' did not your mafter buy you?' I
confeffed he did. ' But I have ferved
' him,' faid I, ' many years, and he has
' taken all my wages and prize-money,
' for I only got one fixpence during the
' war, befides this I have been bap-
' tized, and by the laws of the land
' no man has a right to fell me ' And
I added, that I had heard a lawyer and
others at different times tell my mafter
fo. They both then faid that thofe
people who told me fo were not my
friends, but I replied—' It was very
' extraordinary that other people did
' not know the law as well as they.'
Upon this Captain Doran faid I talked too much Englifh, and if I did
not behave myfelf well, and be quiet,
he had a method on board to make
me I was too well convinced of his
power over me to doubt what he faid;

and

and my former sufferings in the slave-
ship presenting themselves to my mind,
the recollection of them made me
shudder. However, before I retired
I told them that as I could not get
any right among men here I hoped I
should hereafter in Heaven, and I immediately left the cabin, filled with resentment and sorrow. The only coat I
had with me my master took away with
him, and said, "If your prize-money
'had been 10,000l. I had a right to
'it all, and would have taken it.' I had
about nine guineas, which, during my
long sea-faring life, I had scraped together from trifling perquisites and
little ventures, and I hid it that instant,
left my master should take that from
me likewise, still hoping that by some
means or other I should make my
escape to the shore; and indeed some
of my old ship-mates told me not to
despair,

defpair, for they would get me back again; and that, as foon as they could get their pay, they would immediately come to Portfmouth to me, where this fhip was going but, alas! all my hopes were baffled, and the hour of my deliverance was as yet far off. My mafter, having foon concluded his bargain with the captain, came out of the cabin, and he and his people got into the boat and put off, I followed them with aching eyes as long as I could, and when they were out of fight I threw myfelf on the deck, with a heart ready to burft with forrow and anguifh.

CHAP.

C H A P. V.

*The author's reflections on his situation—Is
 treacherously promised of being delivered
 —His despair at sailing for the West
 Indies—Arrives at Montserrat, when
 he is sold to Mr. King—Various interesting instances of oppression, cruelty,
 and extortion, which the author saw
 practiced upon the slaves in the West Indies during his captivity from the year
 1763 to 1766—Address on it to the
 planters.*

Thus, at the moment I expected all
my toils to end, was I plunged, as I
supposed, in a new slavery, in compa-
rison of which all my service hitherto
had

had been perfect freedom, and whofe horrors, always prefent to my mind, now rufhed on it with tenfold aggravation. I wept very bitterly for fome time and began to think that I muft have done fomething to difpleafe the Lord, that he thus punifhed me fo feverely. This filled me with painful reflections on my paft conduct, I recollected that on the morning of our arrival at Deptford I had rafhly fworn that as foon as we reached London I would fpend the day in rambling and fport. My confcience fmote me for this unguarded expreffion: I felt that the Lord was able to difappoint me in all things, and immediately confidered my prefent fituation as a judgment of Heaven on account of my prefumption in fwearing I therefore, with contrition of heart, acknowledged my tranfgreffion to God, and poured out my my foul before him with unfeigned repentance, and with earneft fupplications, I befought him not to abandon me in my diftrefs, nor caft me from his mercy for ever. In a little time my grief, fpent with its own violence, began to fubfide; and after the fiift confufion of my thoughts was over I reflected with more calmnefs on my prefent condition. I confidered that trials and difappointments are fometimes for our good, and I thought God might perhaps have permitted this in order to teach me wifdom and refignation; for he had hitherto fhadowed me with the wings of his mercy, and by his invifible but powerful hand brought me the way I knew not. Thefe reflections gave me a little comfort, and I rofe at laft from the deck with dejection and forrow in my countenance, yet mixed with fome faint hope that

the

the *Lord would appear* for my deliverance.

Soon afterwards, as my new master
was going on shore, he called me to him,
and told me to behave myself well, and
do the business of the ship the same as
any of the rest of the boys, and that I
should fare the better for it, but I
made him no answer. I was then asked
if I could swim, and I said, No, However I was made to go under the
deck, and was well watched. The
next tide the ship got under way,
and soon after arrived at the Mother
Bank, Portfmouth, where she waited a
few days for some of the West India
convoy. While I was here I tried
every means I could devife amongst
the people of the ship to get me a boat
from the shore, as there was none fuffered to come alongfide of the ship;
and their own, whenever it was ufed,

was

was hoifted in again immediately. A failor on board took a guinea from me on pretence of getting me a boat, and promifed me, time after time, that it was hourly to come off. When he had the watch upon deck I watched alfo; and looked long enough, but all in vain, I could never fee either the boat or my guinea again. And what I thought was ftill the worft of all, the fellow gave information, as I afterwards found, all the while to the mates, of my intention to go off, if I could in any way do it, but, rogue like, he never told them he had got a guinea from me to procure my efcape. However, after we had failed, and his trick was made known to the fhip's crew, I had fome fatisfaction in feeing him detefted and delpifed by them all for his behaviour to me. I was ftill in hopes that my old fhipmates would not

not forget heir promife to come for me to Portfmouth· and, indeed, at laſt, but not till the day before we failed, fome of them did come there, and fent me off fome oranges, and other tokens of their regard They alfo fent me word they would come off to me themfelves the next day or the day after; and a lady alfo, who lived in Gofport, wrote to me that fhe would come and take me out of the fhip at the fame time. This lady had been once very intimate with my former mafter. I ufed to fell and take care of a great deal of property for her, in different fhips; and in return fhe always fhewed great friendfhip for me, and ufed to tell my mafter that fhe would take me away to live with her· but, un‐ fortunately for me, a difagreement foon afterwards took place between them; and fhe was fucceeded in my mafter's

good

good graces by another lady, who appeared the mistress of the Ætna, and was lodged on board. I was not so great a favourite with this lady as with the former, she had conceived a pique against me on some occasion when she was on board, and she did not fail to instigate my master to treat me in the manner he did*.

However, the next morning, the 30th of December, the wind being brisk and easterly, the Ætolus frigate, which was to escort the convoy, made a signal for sailing. All the ships

* Thus was I sacrificed to the envy and resentment of this woman for knowing that the lady whom she had succeeded in my master's good graces designed to take me into her service, which, had I once got on shore, she would not have been able to prevent. She felt her pride alarmed at the superiority of her rival in being attended by a black servant it was not less to prevent this than to be revenged on me, that she caused the captain to treat me thus cruelly.

then

then got up their anchors; and, before any of my friends had an opportunity to come off to my relief, to
my inexpressible anguish our ship had
got under way. What tumultuous
emotions agitated my soul when the
convoy got under sail, and I a prisoner
on board, now without hope! I kept
my swimming eyes upon the land in
a state of unutterable grief, not knowing what to do, and despairing how
to help myself. While my mind was
in this situation the fleet sailed on, and
in one days time I lost sight of the
wished-for land. In the first expres-
sions of my grief I reproached my fate,
and wished I had never been born.
I was ready to curse the tide that bore
us, the gale that wafted my prison,
and even the ship that conducted us;
and I called on death to relieve me
from the horrors I felt and dreaded,
that

that I might be in that place

"Where flaves are free and men oppress no more,
"Fool that I was, and fo long to pain,
"To truft to hope, or dream of joy again.
" * * * * * * * * * * * * * *
"Now dragg'd once more beyond the weftern main,
"To groan beneath fome baftard planter's chain,
"Where my poor countrymen in bondage wait
"The long enfranchifement of a ling ring fate.
"Hard ling ring fate! while, ere the dawn of day,
"Rous'd by the lafh they go their cheerlefs way,
"And as their foul with fhame and anguifh burn,
"Salute with groans unwelcome morn's return,
"And, curfing every hour the flow-pic'd fun,
"Purfue their toils till all his race is run
"No eye to mark their fufferings with a tear,
"No friend to comfort, and no hope to cheer.
"Then, like the dull unpity'd brutes, repair
"To ftalls as wretched and as courfe a fare;
"Thank heaven one day of mis'ry was o'er,
"Then fink to fleep, and wifh to wake no more‡.

‡ "The Dying Negro," a poem originally publifhed in
1773 Perhaps it may not be deemed impertinent here to
add, that this elegant and pathetic poem was occa-
fioned, as appears by the advertifement prefixed to it, by
the following incident "A black, who, a few days before
had run away from his mafter, and got himfelf chriftened,
with intent to marry a white woman his fellow-fervant, being taken and fent on board a fhip in the Thames, took an
opportunity of fhooting himfelf through the head "

The

The turbulence of my emotions however naturally gave way to calmer
thoughts, and I soon perceived what
fate had decreed no mortal on earth
could prevent. The convoy sailed on
without any accident, with a pleasant
gale and smooth sea, for six weeks, till
February, when one morning the Æolus
ran down a brig, one of the convoy,
and she instantly went down and was
ingulfed in the dark recesses of the
ocean The convoy was immediately
thrown into great confusion till it was
day-light, and the Æolus was illu-
mined with lights to prevent any far-
ther mischief. On the 13th of February 1763, from the mast head, we defcried our destined island Montserrat:
and soon after I beheld those

" Regions of sorrow, doleful shades, where peace
" And rest can rarely dwell   Hope never comes
" That comes to all, but torture without end
" Still urges."

At

At the fight of this land of bondage, a frefh horror ran through all my frame, and chilled me to the heart. My former flavery now rofe in dreadful review to my mind, and difplayed nothing but mifery, ftripes, and chains; and, in the firft paroxyfm of my grief, I called upon God's thunder, and his avenging power, to direct the ftroke of death to me, rather than permit me to become a flave, and be fold from lord to lord.

In this ftate of my mind our fhip came to an anchor, and foon after difcharged her cargo. I now knew what it was to work hard; I was made to help to unload and load the fhip. And, to comfort me in my diftrefs in that time, two of the failors robbed me of all my money, and ran away from the fhip. I had been fo long ufed to an European climate, that at

3   firft

firſt I felt the ſcorching Weſt India ſun very painful, while the daſhing ſurf would tofs the boat and the people in it frequently above high water mark. Sometimes our limbs were broken with this, or even attended with inſtant death, and I was day by day mangled and torn.

About the middle of May, when the ſhip was got ready to ſail for England, I all the time believing that Fate's blackeſt clouds were gathering over my head, and expecting their burſting would mix me with the dead, Captain Doran ſent for me aſhore one morning, and I was told by the meſſenger that my fate was then determined. With trembling ſteps and fluttering heart I came to the captain, and found with him one Mr. Robert King, a quaker, and the firſt merchant in the place. The captain then told

me

me my former mafter had fent me there to be fold; but that he had defired him to get me the beft mafter he could, as he told him I was a very deferving boy, which Captain Doran faid he found to be true, and if he were to ftay in the Weft Indies he would be glad to keep me himfelf, but he could not venture to take me to London, for he was very fure that when I came there I would leave him. I at that inftant burft out a crying, and begged much of him to take me to England with him, but all to no purpofe. He told me he had got me the very beft mafter in the whole ifland, with whom I fhould be as happy as if I were in England, and for that reafon he chofe to let him have me, though he could fell me to his own brother-in-law for a great deal more money than what he got from this gentleman.

2 Mr.

Mr. King, my new mafter, then made
a reply, and faid the reafon he had
bought me was on account of my good
character; and, as he had not the leaft
doubt of my good behaviour, I fhould
be very well off with him. He alfo
told me he did not live in the Weft
Indies, but at Philadelphia, where he
was going foon; and, as I underftood
fomething of the rules of arithmetic,
when we got there he would put me to
fchool, and fit me for a clerk. This
converfation relieved my mind a little,
and I left thofe gentlemen confiderably
more at eafe in myfelf than when I
came to them; and I was very thank-
ful to Captain Doran, and even to my
old mafter, for the character they had
given me, a character which I afterwards found of infinite fervice to me.
I went on board again, and took leave
of all my fhipmates, and the next day

the ſhip ſailed. When ſhe weighed anchor I went to the waterſide and looked at her with a very wiſhful and aching heart, and followed her with my eyes until ſhe was totally out of ſight. I was ſo bowed down with grief that I could not hold up my head for many months; and if my new maſter had not been kind to me I believe I ſhould have died under it at laſt. And indeed I ſoon found that he fully deſerved the good character which Captain Doran had given me of him, for he poſſeſſed a moſt amiable diſpoſition and temper, and was very charitable and humane. If any of his ſlaves behaved amiſs he did not beat or uſe them ill, but parted with them. This made them afraid of diſobliging him, and as he treated his ſlaves better than any other man on the iſland, ſo he was better and more faithfully ſerved

by them in return. By this kind treatment I did at laft endeavour to compofe myfelf, and with fortitude, though
moneylefs, determined to face whatever fate had decreed for me. Mr.
King foon afked me what I could do;
and at the fame time faid he did not
mean to treat me as a common flave.
I told him I knew fomething of fea-
manfhip, and could fhave and drefs
hair pretty well; and I could refine
wines, which I had learned on fhipboard, where I had once done it, and
that I could write, and underftood
arithmetic tolerably well as far as
the Rule of Three. He then afked
me if I knew any thing of gauging;
and, on my anfwering that I did not,
he faid one of his clerks fhould teach
me to guage.

Mr King dealt in all manner of
merchandize, and kept from one to

six clerks. He loaded many veffels in
a year; particularly to Philadelphia,
where he was born, and was connected
with a great mercantile houfe in that
city. He had befides many veffels
and droggers, of different fizes, which
ufed to go about the ifland; and others
to collect rum, fugar, and other goods.
I underftood pulling and managing
thofe boats very well, and this hard
work, which was the firft that he fet
me to, in the fugar feafons ufed to be
my conftant employment. I have
rowed the boat, and flaved at the
oars, from one hour to fixteen in the
twenty-four; during which I had fifteen pence fterling per day to live on,
though fometimes only ten pence
However this was confiderably more
than was allowed to other flaves that
ufed to work often with me, and belonged to other gentlemen on the
ifland.

island : thofe poor fouls had never more than nine-pence per day, and feldom more than fix-pence, from their mafters or owners, though they earned them three or four pifterines * : for it is a common practice in the Weft Indies for men to purchafe flaves though they have not plantations them-felves, in order to let them out to planters and merchants at fo much a piece by the day, and they give what allowance they chufe out of this pro-duce of their daily work to their flaves for fubfiftence , this allowance is often very fcanty. My mafter often gave the owners of thefe flaves two and a half of thefe pieces per day, and found the poor fellows in victuals himfelf, be-caufe he thought their owners did not feed them well enough according to the

* Thefe pifterines are of the value of a fhilling.

K 3   work

work they did. The flaves ufed to like
this very well; and, as they knew my
mafter to be a man of feeling, they
were always glad to work for him
in preference to any other gentleman,
fome of whom after they had been
paid for thefe poor people's labours,
would not give them their allowance
out of it. Many times have I even
feen thefe unfortunate wretches beaten
for afking for their pay, and often
feverely flogged by their owners if
they did not bring them their daily
or weekly money exactly to the time;
though the poor creatures were obliged
to wait on the gentlemen they had
worked for fometimes for more than
half the day before they could get
their pay; and this generally on Sun-
days, when they wanted the time for
themfelves. In particular, I knew a
countryman of mine who once did not
                                    bring

bring the weekly money directly that
it was earned; and though he brought
it the fame day to his mafter, yet he
was ftaked to the ground for his pre-
tended negligence, and was juft going
to receive a hundred lafhes, but for
a gentleman who begged him off fifty.
This poor man was very induftrious;
and, by his frugality, had faved fo
much money by working on fhipboard,
that he had got a white man to buy
him a boat, unknown to his mafter.
Some time after he had this little
eftate, the governor wanted a boat to
bring his fugar from different parts of
the ifland, and, knowing this to be a
negro-man's boat, he feized upon it
for himfelf, and would not pay the
owner a farthing. The man on this
went to his mafter, and complained
to him of this act of the governor;
but the only fatisfaction he received

was

was to be damned very heartily by his master, who asked him how dare any of his negroes to have a boat. If the justly-merited ruin of the governor's fortune could be any gratification to the poor man he had thus robbed, he was not without consolation. Extortion and rapine are poor providers; and some time after this the governor died in the King's Bench in England, as I was told, in great poverty. The last war favoured this poor negro-man, and he found some means to escape from his Christian master: he came to England; where I saw him afterwards several times. Such treatment as this often drives these miserable wretches to despair, and they run away from their masters at the hazard of their lives. Many of them, in this place, unable to get their pay when they have earned it, and fear-

ing

ing to be flogged, as ufual, if they return home without it, run away where they can for fhelter, and a reward is often offered to bring them in dead or alive. My mafter ufed fometimes, in thefe cafes, to agree with their owners, and to fettle with them himfelf; and thereby he faved many of them a flogging.

Once, for a few days, I was let out to fit a veffel, and I had no victuals allowed me by either party, at laft I told my mafter of this treatment, and he took me away from it. In many of the eftates, on the different iflands where I ufed to be fent for rum or fugar, they would not deliver it to me, or any other negro; he was therefore obliged to fend a white man along with me to thofe places; and then he ufed to pay him from fix to ten pistarines a day. From being thus em-

ploved, during the time I served Mr.
King, in going about the different
estates on the island, I had all the opportunity I could wish for to see the
dreadful usage of the poor men; usage
that reconciled me to my situation,
and made me blefs God for the hands
into which I had fallen.

I had the good fortune to pleafe my
master in every department in which
he employed me; and there was
scarcely any part of his businefs, or
houfhold affairs, in which I was not
occafionally engaged. I often supplied the place of a clerk, in receiving
and delivering cargoes to the ships, in
tending stores, and delivering goods.
and, besides this, I used to shave and
drefs my master when convenient, and
take care of his horfe, and when it
was necefsary, which was very often,
I worked likewife on board of different
veffels

veffels of his. By thefe means I became very ufeful to my mafter; and
faved him, as he ufed to acknowledge,
above a hundred pounds a year. Nor
did he fcruple to fay I was of more advantage to him than any of his clerks;
though their ufual wages in the Weft
Indies are from fixty to a hundred
pounds current a year.

I have fometimes heard it afferted
that a negro cannot earn his mafter
the firft coft, but nothing can be further from the truth. I fuppofe nine
tenths of the mechanics throughout
the Weft Indies are negro flaves, and
I well know the coopers among them
earn two dollars a day; the carpenters
the fame, and oftentimes more, as
alfo the mafons, fmiths, and fifher-
men, &c. and I have known many
flaves whofe mafters would not take
a thoufand pounds current for them.

But

But furely this affertion refutes itfelf, for, if it be true, why do the planters and merchants pay fuch a price for flaves? And, above all, why do thofe who make this affertion exclaim the moft loudly againft the abolition of the flave trade? So much are men blinded, and to fuch inconfiftent arguments are they driven by miftaken intereft! I grant, indeed, that flaves are fome times, by half-feeding, half-clothing, over-working and ftripes, reduced fo low, that they are turned out as unfit for fervice, and left to perifh in the woods, or expire on a dunghill.

My mafter was feveral times offered by different gentlemen one hundred guineas for me, but he always told them he would not fell me, to my great joy: and I ufed to double my diligence and care for fear of getting into the hands of thofe men who did not allow a valuable flave the common support of life. Many of them even used to find fault with my mafter for feeding his flaves fo well as he did; although I often went hungry, and an Englifhman might think my fare very indifferent; but he ufed to tell them he always would do it, becaufe the flaves thereby looked better and did more work.

While I was thus employed by my mafter I was often a witnefs to cruelties of every kind, which were exercifed on my unhappy fellow flaves. I ufed frequently to have different cargoes of new negroes in my care for fale, and it was almoft a conftant practice with our clerks, and other whites, to commit violent depredations on the chaftity of the female flaves, and thefe I was, though with reluctance, obliged to fubmit to at all times, being unable to help

help them. When we have had some
of these slaves on board my master's
vessels to carry them to other islands,
or to America, I have known our mates
to commit these acts most shamefully,
to the disgrace, not of Christians only,
but of men. I have even known them
gratify their brutal passion with females
not ten years old; and these abomi-
nations some of them practised to such
scandalous excess, that one of our captains discharged the mate and others
on that account. And yet in Montferrat I have seen a negro man staked
to the ground, and cut most shock-
ingly, and then his ears cut off bit by
bit, because he had been connected
with a white woman who was a common prostitute. as if it were no crime
in the whites to rob an innocent African girl of her virtue; but most heinous in a black man only to gratify a
                                    passion

paſſion of nature, where the temptation was offered by one of a different colour, though the moſt abandoned woman of her ſpecies.

One Mr. D——— told me that he had ſold 41000 negroes, and that he once cut off a negro-man's leg for running away———I aſked him if the man had died in the operation, how he as a chriſtian could anſwer for the horrid act before God? and he told me, anſwering was a thing of another world; what he thought and did were policy. I told him that the chriſtian doctrine taught us to do unto others as we would that others ſhould do unto us. He then ſaid that his ſcheme had the deſired effect—it cured that man and ſome others of running away.

Another negro-man was half hanged, and then burnt, for attempting to poi-

ſon

fon a cruel overfeer. Thus by re-
peated cruelties are the wretched firft
urged to defpair, and then murdered,
becaufe they ftill retain fo much of human nature about them as to wifh to
put an end to their mifery, and retali-
ate on their tyrants! Thefe overfeers
are indeed for the moft part perfons of
the worft character of any denomination of men in the Weft Indies Unfortunately, many humane gentlemen,
by not refiding on their eftates, are
obliged to leave the management of
them in the hands of thefe human
butchers, who cut and mangle the
flaves in a fhocking manner on the
moft trifling occafions, and altogether
treat them in every refpect like brutes.
They pay no regard to the fituation of
pregnant women, nor the leaft attention to the lodging of the field negroes.
Their huts, which ought to be well covered, and the place dry where they
take

take their little repofe, are often open
fheds, built in damp places; fo that,
when the poor creatures return tired
from the toils of the field, they con-
tract many diforders, from being expofed to the damp air in this uncom-
fortable ftate, while they are heated,
and their pores are open. This neg-
lect certainly confpires with many
others to caufe a decreafe in the births
as well as in the lives of the grown
negroes. I can quote many inftances
of gentlemen who refide on their
eftates in the weft Indies, and then
the fcene is quite changed; the negroes are treated with lenity and proper care, by which their lives are pro-
longed, and their mafters profited.
To the honour of humanity, I knew
feveral gentlemen who managed their
eftates in this manner; and they found
that benevolence was their true inte--
reft.

reft. And, among many I could mention in feveral of the iflands, I knew one in Montferrat * whofe flaves looked remarkably well, and never needed any frefh fupplies of negroes; and there are many other eftates, efpecially in Barbadoes, which, from fuch judicious treatment, need no frefh ftock of negroes at any time. I have the honour of knowing a moft worthy and humane gentleman, who is a native of Barbadoes, and has eftates there †. This gentleman has wrote a treatife on the ufage of his own flaves. He allows them two hours for refhment at mid-day; and many other indulgencies and comforts, particularly in their lying, and, befides this, he raifes more provifions on his eftate than they can deftroy, fo that by thefe attentions

* Mr. Dubury, and many others, Montferrat.
† Sir Philip Gibbes, Baronet, Barbadoes.

he

he faves the lives of his negroes, and keeps them healthy, and as happy as the condition of flavery can admit. I myfelf, as fhall appear in the fequel, managed an eftate, wheie, by thofe attentions, the negioes were uncommonly cheerful and healthy, and did more work by half than by the common mode of treatment they ufually do. Foi want, theiefore, of fuch caie and attention to the poor negroes, and otherwife oppreffed as they are, it is no wonder that the decreafe fhould iequire 20,000 new negroes annually to fill up the vacant places of the dead.

Even in Barbadoes, notwithftanding thofe humane exceptions which I have mentioned, and others I am acquainted with, which juftly make it quoted as a place where flaves meet with the beft treatment, and need feweft recruits of any in the Weft Indies, yet this
ifland

island requires 1000 negroes annually to keep up the original stock, which is only 80,000. So that the whole term of a negro's life may be said to be there but sixteen years *? And yet the climate here is in every respect the same as that from which they are taken, except in being more wholesome. Do the British colonies decrease in this manner? And yet what a prodigious difference is there between an English and West India climate?

While I was in Montferrat I knew a negro man, named Emanuel Sankey, who endeavoured to escape from his miserable bondage, by concealing himself on board of a London ship: but fate did not favour the poor oppressed man; for, being discovered when the vessel was under sail, he was delivered up again to his master. This *Christian*

* Benezet's Account of Guinea, p. 16.

master

master immediately pinned the wretch down to the ground at each wrist and ancle, and then took fome fticks of fealing wax, and lighted them, and dropped it all over his back. There was another mafter who was noted for cruelty; and I believe he had not a flave but what had been cut, and had pieces fairly taken out of the flefh and after they had been punifhed thus, he ufed to make them get into a long wooden box or cafe he had for that purpofe, in which he fhut them up during pleafure. It was juft about the height and breadth of a man; and the poor wretches had no room, when in the cafe to move.

It was very common in feveral of the iflands, particulaly in St. Kitt's, for the flaves to be branded with the initial letters of their mafter's name; and a load of heavy iron hooks hung about their necks. Indeed on the moft

trifling

trifling occasions they were loaded with chains ; and often inftruments of torture were added The iron muzzle, thumb-fcrews, &c. are fo well known, as not to need a defcription, and were fometimes applied for the flighteft faults. I have feen a negro beaten till fome of his bones were broken, for only letting a pot boil over. Is it furprifing that ufage like this fhould drive the poor creatures to defpair, and make them feek a refuge in death from thofe evils which render their lives intolerable—while,

" With fhudd ring horror pale, and eyes aghaft,
" They view their lamentable lot, and find
" No reft!"

This they frequently do. A negro-man on board a veffel of my mafter, while I belonged to her, having been put in irons for fome trifling mifdemeanor, and kept in that ftate

for

3

for some days, being weary of life, took an opportunity of jumping overboard into the sea, however, he was picked up without being drowned. Another, whose life was also a burden to him, resolved to starve himself to death, and refused to eat any victuals: this procured him a severe flogging: and he also, on the first occasion which offered, jumped overboard at Charles Town, but was saved.

Nor is there any greater regard shewn to the little property than there is to the persons and lives of the negroes I have already related an instance or two of particular oppression out of many which I have witnessed; but the following is frequent in all the islands. The wretched field-slaves, after toiling all the day for an unfeeling owner, who gives them but little victuals, steal sometimes a few moments from

rest

rest or refreshment to gather some small portion of grafs, according as their time will admit. This they commonly tie up in a parcel; either a bit's worth (six-pence) or half a bit's worth; and bring it to town, or to the market, to sell. Nothing is more common than for the white people on this occasion to take the grafs from them without paying for it; and not only so, but too often also, to my knowledge, our clerks, and many others, at the same time have committed acts of violence on the poor, wretched, and helplefs females, whom I have seen for hours stand crying to no purpose, and get no redrefs or pay of any kind. Is not this one common and crying sin enough to bring down God's judgment on the islands? He tells us the oppreffor and the oppreffed are both in his hands; and if thefe are not the

poor,

poor, the broken-hearted, the blind, the captive, the bruised, which our Saviour speaks of, who are they? One of these depredators once, in St. Eustatia, came on board of our vessel, and bought some fowls and pigs of me; and a whole day after his departure with the things, he returned again and wanted his money back. I refused to give it; and, not seeing my captain on board, he began the common pranks with me; and swore he would even break open my chest and take my money. I therefore expected, as my captain was absent, that he would be as good as his word and he was just proceeding to strike me, when fortunately a British seaman on board, whose heart had not been debauched by a West India climate, interposed and prevented him. But had the cruel man struck me I certainly should have defended

myself at the hazard of my life; for
what is life to a man thus oppreſſed?
He went away, however, ſwearing, and
threatened that whenever he caught me
on ſhore he would ſhoot me, and pay
for me afterwards.

The ſmall account in which the life
of a negro is held in the Weſt Indies,
is ſo univerſally known, that it might
ſeem impertinent to quote the following extract, if ſome people had not
been hardy enough of late to aſſert
that negroes are on the ſame footing in
that reſpect as Europeans.   By the
329th Act, page 125, of the Aſſembly
of Barbadoes, it is enacted ‘ That if
‘ any negro, or other ſlave, under pu-
‘ niſhment by his maſter, or his order,
‘ for running away, or any other crime
‘ or miſdemeanor towards his ſaid
‘ maſter, unfortunately ſhall ſuffer in
‘ life or member, no perſon what-
‘ ſo-

'foever shall be liable to a fine; but
'if any man shall out of *wantonnefs*,
'or only of *bloody-mindednefs*, or *cruel*
'*intention, wilfully kill a negro, or other*
'*flave, of his own, he shall pay into the*
'*public treasury fifteen pounds sterling.*'
And it is the fame in moft, if not all,
of the Weft India iflands. Is not this
one of the many acts of the iflands
which call loudly for redrefs? And
do not the Affembly which enacted it
deferve the appellation of favages and
brutes rather than of chriftians and
men? It is an act at once unmerciful,
unjuft, and unwife, which for cruelty
would difgrace an affembly of thofe
who are called barbarians, and for its
injuftice and *infanity* would fhock the
morality and common fenfe of a Same de or Hottentot.

Shocking as this and many more acts
of the bloody Weft India code at firft

view

view appear, how is the iniquity of it
heightened when we confider to whom
it may be extended! Mr. James Tobin,
a zealous labourer in the vineyard of
flavery gives an account of a French
planter of his acquaintance, in the
ifland of Martinico, who fhewed him
many mulattoes working in the fields
like beafts of burden, and he told Mr
Tobin thefe were all the produce of his
own loins! And I myfelf have known
fimilar inftances.   Pray, reader, are
thefe fons and daughters of the French
planter lefs his children by being begotten on black women? And what
muft be the virtue of thofe legiflators,
and the feelings of thofe fathers, who
eftimate the lives of their fons, however begotten, at no more than fifteen pounds, though they fhould be
murdered, as the act fays, *out of wantonnefs and bloody-mindednefs!* But is

not

not the flave trade entirely a war with the heart of man? And furely that which is begun by breaking down the barriers of virtue involves in its continuance deftruction to every principle, and buries all fentiments in ruin!

I have often feen flaves, particularly thofe who were meagre, in different iflands, put into fcales and weighed, and then fold from three pence to five pence or nine pence a pound. My mafter, however, whofe humanity was fhocked at this mode, ufed to fell fuch by the lump. And at or after a fale it was not uncommon to fee negroes taken from their wives, wives taken from their hufbands, and children from their parents, and fent off to other iflands, and wherever elfe their mercilefs lords choofe, and probably never more during life fee each other! Oftentimes my heart has bled at thefe

L 3   partings;

partings, when the friends of the departed have been at the water side, and, with sighs and tears, have kept their eyes fixed on the vessel, till it went out of fight.

A poor Creole negro I knew well, who, after having been often thus transported from island to island, at laft resided in Montserrat. This man used to tell me many melancholy tales of himself. Generally, after he had done working for his master, he used to employ his few leisure moments to go a fishing. When he had caught any fish, his master would frequently take them from him without paying him; and at other times some other white people would serve him in the same manner. One day he said to me, very movingly, ' Sometimes when a ' white man take away my fish I go to ' my mafer, and he get me my right; ' and

'and when my mafer by ftrength take
'away my fifhes, what me muft do?'
'I can t go to any body to be righted;
'then,' faid the poor man, looking up
above, 'I muft look up to God Mighty
'in the top for right.' This artlefs
tale moved me much, and I could not
help feeling the juft caufe Mofes had
in redreffing his brother againft the
Egyptian. I exhorted the man to look
up ftill to the God on the top, fince
there was no redrefs below. Though
I little thought then that I myfelf fhould
more than once experience fuch impofition, and need the fame exhortation
hereafter, in my own tranfactions in
the iflands; and that even this poor
man and I fhould fome time after fuffer
together in the fame manner, as fhall
be related hereafter.

Nor was fuch ufage as this confined
to particular places or individuals; for,

in

in all the different islands in which I have been (and I have visited no less than fifteen) the treatment of the slave was nearly the same, so nearly indeed, that the history of an island, or even a plantation, with a few such exceptions as I have mentioned, might serve for a history of the whole. Such a tendency has the slave-trade to debauch men's minds, and harden them to every feeling of humanity! For I will not suppose that the dealers in slaves are born worse than other men—No; it is the fatality of this mistaken avarice, that it corrupts the milk of human kindness and turns it into gall. And, had the pursuits of those men been different, they might have been as generous, as tender-hearted and just, as they are unfeeling, rapacious and cruel. Surely this traffic cannot be good, which spreads like a pestilence, and taints what it touches! which violates

violates that first natural right of man-
kind, equality and independency, and
gives one man a dominion over his
fellows which God could never intend!
For it raises the owner to a state as far
above man as it depresses the slave below it; and, with all the presumption
of human pride, sets a distinction between them, immeasurable in extent,
and endless in duration! Yet how mistaken is the avarice even of the planter.
Are slaves more useful by being thus
humbled to the condition of brutes, than
they would be if suffered to enjoy the pri-
vileges of men? The freedom which
diffuses health and prosperity throughout Britain answers you—No. When
you make men slaves you deprive them
of half their virtue, you set them in
your own conduct an example of fraud,
rapine, and cruelty, and compel them
to live with you in a state of war, and

L 5   yet

yet you complain that they are not honeft or faithful! You ftupify them with
ftripes, and think it neceffary to keep
them in a ftate of ignorance; and yet
you affert that they are incapable of
learning; that their minds are fuch
a barren foil or moor, that culture
would be loft on them, and that they
come from a climate, where nature,
though prodigal of her bounties in a
degree unknown to yourfelves, has left
man alone fcant and unfinifhed, and
incapable of enjoying the treafures
fhe has poured out for him!--An affertion at once impious and abfurd
Why do you ufe thofe inftruments of
torture? Are they fit to be applied by
one rational being to another? And
are ye not ftruck with fhame and mortification, to fee the partakers of your
nature reduced fo low? But, above all,
are there no dangers attending this
mode

mode of treatment? Are you not hourly in dread of an insurrection? Nor would it be surprising. for when

" ————No peace is given
" To us enslav'd but custody severe,
" And stripes and arbitrary punishment
" Inflicted—What peace can we return ?
" But to our power, hostility and hate,
" Untam'd reluctance, and revenge, though flow.
" Yet ever plotting how the conqueror least
" May reap his conquest, and may least rejoice
" In doing what we most in suffering feel."

But by changing your conduct, and treating your slaves as men, every cause of fear would be banished. They would be faithful, honest, intelligent and vigorous; and peace, prosperity,. and happiness, would attend you.

CHAP. VI.

Some account of Brimstone-Hill in Mont-
serrat—Favourable change in the au-
thor's situation—He commences merchant
with three pence—His various success in
dealing in the different islands, and Ame-
rica, and the impositions he meets with in
his transactions with Europeans—A cu-
rious imposition on human nature—Dan-
ger of the surfs in the West Indies—
Remarkable instance of kidnapping a free
mulatto—The author is nearly murdered
by Doctor Perkins in Savannah.

In the precedeing chapter I have set
before the reader a few of thofe many
inftances of oppreffion, extortion, and
cruelty, which I have been a witnefs

2   to

to in the West Indies but, were I to enumerate them all, the catalogue would be tedious and difgufting. The punifhments of the flaves on every trifling occafion are fo frequent, and fo well known together with the different inftruments with which they are tortured, that it cannot any longer afford novelty to recite them; and they are too fhocking to yield delight either to the writer or the reader. I fhall therefore hereafter only mention fuch as incidentally befell myfelf in the courfe of my adventures.

In the variety of departments in which I was employed by my mafter, I had an opportunity of feeing many curious fcenes in different iflands; but, above all, I was ftruck with a celebrated curiofity called Brimftone-Hill, which is a high and fteep mountain, fome few miles from the town of Plymouth in Montferrat. I had often heard of fome

wonders

. . . . this
. . . . white.
. . . . When we
. . . . , . . nder different
. . . . . . brimſtone, occa-
. . . . . . ams of various little
. . . . . . were then boiling natu-
ra'l. in t . earth. Some of theſe ponds
were as white as milk, ſome quite
blue, and many others of different colours. I had taken ſome potatoes with
me, and I put them into different ponds,
and in a few minutes they were well
boiled. I taſted ſome of them, but they
were very ſulphurous; and the ſilver
ſhoe buckles, and all the other things
of that metal we had among us, were,
in a little time turned as black as lead.

Some time in the year 1763, kind Providence ſeemed to appear rather more
favourable to me. One of my maſter's
veſſels, a Bermudas ſloop, about ſixty
tons burthen was commanded by one
Captain

Captain Thomas Farmer, an Eng . .
man, a very alert and active man, . .
gained my master a great deal of r .
ney by his good management in car
ing paffengers from one ifland to another, but very often his failors ufed to
get drunk and run away from the veffel,
which hindered him in his bufinefs very
much. This man had taken a liking to
me ; and many different times begged
of my mafter to let me go a trip with
him as a failor, but he would tell him
he could not fpare me, though the veffel fometimes could not go for want of
hands, for failors were generally very
fcarce in the ifland. However, at laft,
from neceffity or force, my mafter was
prevailed on, though very reluctantly,
to let me go with this captain, but he
gave him great charge to take care that
I did not run away, for if I did he
would make him pay for me. This
being the cafe, the captain had for
fome

some time a sharp eye upon me whenever the vessel anchored; and as soon
as she returned I was sent for on shore
again. Thus was I slaving as it were
for life, sometimes at one thing, and
sometimes at another; so that the captain and I were nearly the most useful
men in my master's employment. I
also became so useful to the captain
on shipboard, that many times, when
he used to ask for me to go with him,
though it should be but for twenty-
four hours, to some of the islands near
us, my master would answer he could
not spare me, at which the captain
would swear, and would not go the trip;
and tell my master I was better to him
on board than any three white men he
had, for they used to behave ill in
many respects, particularly in getting
drunk; and then they frequently got
the boat stove, so as to hinder the vessel from coming back as soon as she
might

might have done. This my mafter
knew very well; and at laft, by the
captain's conftant entreaties, after
I had been feveral times with him,
one day to my great joy, told me
the captain would not let him reft,
and afked whether I would go aboard
as a failor, or ftay on fhore and mind
the ftores, for he could not bear any
longer to be plagued in this manner.
I was very happy at this propofal, for
I immediately thought I might in time
ftand fome chance by being on board
to get a little money, or poffibly make
my efcape if I fhould be ufed ill: I
alfo expected to get better food, and in
greater abundance; for I had oftentimes
felt much hunger, though my mafter
treated his flaves, as I have obferved,
uncommonly well. I therefore, without hefitation, anfwered him, that I
would go and be a failor if he pleafed.
Accordingly I was ordered on board
directly.

directly. Nevertheless, between the vessel and the shore, when she was in port, I had little or no reft, as my mafter always wifhed to have me along with him. Indeed he was a very pleafant gentleman, and but for my expectations on fhipboard I fhould not have thought of leaving him. But the captain liked me alfo very much, and I was entirely his right-hand man. I did all I could to deferve his favour, and in return I received better treatment from him than any other I believe ever met with in the Weft Indies in my fituation.

After I had been failing for fome time with this captain, at length I endeavoured to try my luck and commence merchant. I had but a very fmall capital to begin with; for one fingle half bit, which is equal to three-pence in England, made up my whole ftock. However I trufted to the Lord to be

with

with me; and at one of our trips to
St. Euflatia, a Dutch ifland, I bought
a glafs tumbler with my half bit, and
when I came to Montferrat I fold it for
a bit, or fix-pence. Luckily we made
feveral fucceffive trips to St. Euftatia
(which was a general mart for the
Weft Indies, about twenty leagues from
Montferrat) and in our next, finding
my tumbler fo profitable, with this one
bit I bought two tumblers more; and
when I came back I fold them for two
bits equal to a fhilling fterling. When
we went again I bought with thefe two
bits four more of thefe glaffes, which
I fold for fout bits on our return to
Montferrat: and in our next voyage
to St. Euftatia, I bought two glaffes
with one bit, and with the other three
I bought a jug of Geneva, nearly about
three pints in meafure. When we came
to Montferrat, I fold the gin for eight
bits, and the tumblers for two, fo that

my

my capital now amounted in all to a dollar, well hufbanded and acquired in the fpace of a month or fix weeks, when I bleffed the Lord that I was fo rich. As we failed to different iflands, I laid this money out in various things occafionally, and it ufed to turn to very good account, efpecially when we went to Guadaloupe, Grenada, and the reft of the French iflands. Thus was I going all about the iflands upwards of four years, and ever trading as I went, during which I experienced many inftances of ill ufage, and have feen many injuries done to other negroes in our dealings with whites. and, amidft our recications, when we have been dancing and merry-making, they, without caufe, have molefted and in-fulted us Indeed I was more than once obliged to look up to God on high, as I had advifed the poor fifher-man fome time before. And I had not

been

been long trading for myself in the manner I have related above, when I experienced the like trial in company with him as follows. This man being used to the water, was upon an emergency put on board of us by his master to work as another hand, on a voyage to Santa Cruz, and at our sailing he had brought his little all for a venture which consisted of six bits' worth of limes and oranges in a bag; I had also my whole stock, which was about twelve bits' worth of the same kind of goods, separate in two bags, for we had heard these fruits sold well in that island. When we came there, in some little convenient time he and I went ashore with our fruits to sell them; but we had scarcely landed when we were met by two white men, who presently took our three bags from us. We could not at first guess what they meant to do, and for some time we thought they

they were jesting with us, but they too soon let us know otherwise, for they took our ventures immediately to a house hard by, and adjoining the fort, while we followed all the way begging of them to give us our fruits, but in vain. They not only refused to return them but swore at us, and threatened if we did not immediately depart they would flog us well. We told them these three bags were all we were worth in the world, and that we brought them with us to sell when we came from Mont-ferrat, and shewed them the vessel. But this was rather against us, as they now saw we were strangers as well as slaves. They still therefore swore, and desired us to be gone, and even took sticks to beat us; while we, seeing they meant what they said, went off in the greatest confusion and despair. Thus, in the very minute of gaining more by three times than I ever did

by

by any venture in my life before, was
I deprived of every farthing I was
worth. An infupportable misfortune!
but how to help ourfelves we knew
not. In our confternation we went to
the commanding officer of the fort,
and told him how we had been ferved
by fome of his people; but we obtained
not the leaft redrefs. he anfwered our
complaints only by a volley of impre-
cations againft us, and immediately
took a horfe-whip, in order to chaftife
us, fo that we were obliged to turn
out much fafter than we came in. I
now, in the agony of diftrefs and indig-
nation, wifhed that the ire of God in his
forked lightning might transfix thefe
cruel oppreffors among the dead. Still
however we perfevered; went back
again to the houfe, and begged and befought them again and again for our
fruits, till at laft fome other people that
were in the houfe afked if we would be
contented

contented if they kept one bag and gave us the other two. We, feeing no remedy whatever, confented to this, and they, obferving one bag to have both kinds of fruit in it, which belonged to my companion, kept that; and the other two, which were mine they gave us back. As foon as I got them, I ran as faft as I could, and got the firft negro man I could to help me off, my companion, however, ftayed a little longer to plead; he told them the bag they had was his, and likewife all that he was worth in the world; but this was of no avail, and he was obliged to return without it. The poor old man wringing his hands, cried bitterly for his lofs; and, indeed, he then did look up to God on high, which fo moved me with pity for him, that I gave him nearly one third of my fruits. We then proceeded to the markets to fell them; and Providence

was

was more favourable to us than we could have expected, for we fold our fruits uncommonly well; I got for mine about thirty-seven bits. Such a furprising reverse of fortune in fo fhort a fpace of time feemed like a dream, and proved no fmall encouragement for me to truft the Lord in any fituation. My captain afterwards frequently ufed to take my part, and get me my right, when I have been plundered or ufed ill by thefe tender Chriftian depredators; among whom I have fhuddered to obferve the unceafing blafphemous execrations which are wantonly thrown out by perfons of all ages and conditions, not only without occafion, but even as if they were indulgences and pleafure.

At one of our trips to St. Kitt's, I had eleven bits of my own; and my friendly captain lent me five more,

M

with

with which I bought a Bible. I was very glad to get this book, which I fcarcely could meet with any where. I think there was none fold in Montferrat; and, much to my grief, from being forced out of the Ætna in the manner I have related, my Bible, and the Guide to the Indians, the two books I loved above all others, were left behind.

While I was in this place, St. Kitt's, a very curious impofition on human nature took place. — A white man wanted to marry in the church a free black woman that had land and flaves in Montferrat: but the clergy man told him it was againfi the law of the place to marry a white and a black in the church. The man then afked to be married on the water, to which the parfon confented, and the two lovers went in one boat, and the parfon and

2　　　　clerk

clerk in another, and thus the ceremony was performed. After this the loving pair came on board our veffel, and my captain treated them extremely well, and brought them fafe to Montferrat.

The reader cannot but judge of the irkfomenefs of this fituation to a mind like mine, in being daily expofed to new hardfhips and impofitions, after having feen many better days, and been as it were, in a ftate of freedom and plenty, added to which, every part of the world I had hitherto been in, feemed to me a paradife in comparifon of the Weft Indies. My mind was therefore hourly replete with inventions and thoughts of being freed, and, if poffible, by honeft and honourable means, for I always remembered the old adage; and I truft it has ever been my ruling principle, that " Ho-

M 2   " neft

"nefty is the beft policy," and likewife
that other golden precept—"To do
"unto all men as I would they fhould
"do unto me." However, as I was
from early years a predeftinarian, I
thought whatever fate had determined
muft ever come to pafs, and therefore, if ever it were my lot to be freed
nothing could prevent me, although I
fhou'd at prefent fee no means or hope
to obtain my freedom, on the other
hand, if it were my fate not to be freed
I never fhou'd be fo, and all my endeavours for that purpofe would be
fruitlefs. In the midft of thefe thought
I therefore looked up with prayer
anxiously to God for my liberty, and
at the fame time ufed every honeft
means, and did all that was poffible
on my part to obtain it. In procefs of
time I became mafter of a few pound
a different means of making more, who

r, friendly captain knew very well, this occasioned him sometimes to take liberties with me, but whenever he treated me waspishly I used plainly to tell him my mind, and that I would die before I would be imposed upon as other negroes were, and that to me life had lost its relish when liberty was gone. This I said although I foresaw my then well-being or future hopes of freedom (humanly speaking) depended on this man. However, as he could not bear the thoughts of my not feeling with him, he always became mild on my threats. I therefore continued with him; and, from my great attention to his orders and his business, I gained him credit, and through his kindness to me I at last procured my liberty. While I thus went on, filled with the thoughts of freedom, and resisting oppression as well as I was able, my life hung daily

M 3

in

in fufpence, particularly in the furfs I
have formerly mentioned, as I could
not fwim. Thefe are extremely violent
throughout the Weft Indies, and I was
ever expofed to their howling rage and
devouring fury in all the iflands. I
have feen them ftrike and tofs a boat
right up an end, and maim feveral on
board   Once in the Grenada iflands,
when I and about eight others were
pulling a large boat with two pun-
cheons of water in it, a furf ftruck us,
and drove the boat and all in it about
half a ftone's throw, among fome trees,
and above the high water mark.   We
were obliged to get all the affiftance we
could from the neareft eftate to mend the
boat, and launch it into the water again.
At Montferrat one night, in preffing hard
to get off the fhore on board, the punt
was overfet with us four times, the firft
time I was very near being drowned;
however

however the jacket I had on kept me up above water a little fpace of time, while I called on a man near me who was a good fwimmer, and told him I could not fwim ; he then made hafte to me, and, juft as I was finking, he caught hold of me, and brought me to founding, and then he went and brought the punt alfo. As foon as we had turned the water out of her, left we fhould be ufed ill for being abfent, we attempted again three times more, and as often the horrid furfs ferved us as at firft; but at laft, the fifth time we attempted, we gained our point, at the eminent hazard of our lives. One day alfo, at Old Road in Mont-ferrat, our captain, and three men be-fides myfelf, were going in a large canoe in queft of rum and fugar, when a fingle furf toffed the canoe an amazing diftance from the water,

M 4   and

and some of us, near a stone's throw
from each other most of us were very
much bruised, so that I and many
more often said, and really thought,
that there was not such another place
under the heavens as this. I longed
therefore much to leave it, and daily
wished to see my master's promise performed of going to Philadelphia.

While we lay in this place a very cruel
thing happened on board of our sloop
which filled me with horror, though I
found afterwards such practices were
frequent. There was a very clever and
decent free young mulatto-man who
sailed a long time with us: he had a
free woman for his wife, by whom he
had a child, and she was then living
on shore, and all very happy. Our
captain and mate, and other people on
board, and several elsewhere, even the
natives of Bermudas, all knew this
young

young man from a child that he was always free, and no one had ever claimed him as their property. however, as might too often overcomes right in these parts, it happened that a Bermudas captain, whose vessel lay there for a few days in the road, came on board of us, and seeing the mulatto-man, whose name was Joseph Clipson, he told him he was not free, and that he had orders from his master to bring him to Bermudas. The poor man could not believe the captain to be in earnest, but he was very soon unde-ceived, his men laying violent hands on him; and although he shewed a cer-tificate of his being born free at St. Kitt's, and most people on board knew that he served his time to boat-building, and always passed for a free man, yet he was forcibly taken out of our vessel. **He then asked to be**

afhore before the fecretary or magif-
trates, and thefe infernal invaders of
human rights promifed him he fhould,
but, inftead of that, they carried him
on board of the other veffel: and the
next day, without giving the poor man
any hearing on fhore, or fuffering him
even to fee his wife or child, he was
carried away, and probably doomed
never more in this world to fee them
again. Nor was this the only inftance
of this kind of barbarity I was a witnefs to. I have fince often feen in
Jamaica and other iflands, free men,
whom I have known in America, thus
villainoufly trepanned and held in bondage. I have heard of two fimilar practices even in Philadelphia: and were
it not for the benevolence of the quak-
ers in that city, many of the fable race,
who now breathe the air of liberty,
would, I believe, be groaning indeed
under

under fome planter's chains. Thefe things opened my mind to a new fcene of horror to which I had been before a ftranger. Hitherto I had thought only flavery dreadful, but the ftate of a free negro appeared to me now equally fo at leaft, and in fome refpects even worfe, for they live in conftant alarm for their liberty, which is but nominal, for they are univerfally infulted and plundered without the poffibility of redrefs; for fuch is the equity of the Weft Indian laws, that no free negro's evidence will be admitted in their courts of juftice. In this fituation is it furprifing that flaves, when mildly treated, fhould prefer even the mifery of flavery to fuch a mockery of freedom? I was now completely difgufted with the Weft Indies, and thought I never fhould be entirely free until I had left them.

M 6 " With

"With thoughts like these my anxious boding mind
" Recall'd those pleasing scenes I left behind;
" Scenes where fair Liberty in bright array
" Makes darkness bright, and e'en illumines day,
" Where nor complexion, wealth, or station, can
" Protect the wretch who makes a slave of man.'

I determined to make every exertion to obtain my freedom, and to return to Old England. For this purpose I thought a knowledge of navigation might be of use to me, for, though I did not intend to run away unless I should be ill used, yet, in such a case, if I understood navigation, I might attempt my escape in our sloop, which was one of the swiftest sailing vessels in the West Indies, and I could be at no loss for hands to join me and if I should make this attempt, I had intended to have gone for England; but this, as I said, was only to be in the event of my meeting with any ill usage. I

there-

therefore employed the mate of our vessel to teach me navigation, for which I agreed to give him twenty-four dollars, and actually paid him part of the money down; though when the captain, some time after, came to know that the mate was to have such a sum for teaching me, he rebuked him, and said it was a shame for him to take any money from me. However, my progress in this useful art was much retarded by the constancy of our work. Had I wished to run away I did not want opportunities, which frequently presented themselves; and particularly at one time, soon after this. When we were at the island of Gaudeloupe there was a large fleet of merchantmen bound for Old France, and, seamen then being very scarce, they gave from fifteen to twenty pounds a man for the run. Our mate, and all the white sailors, left

left our veffel on this account, and went on board of the French fhips. They would have had me alfo to go with them, for they regarded me, and fwore to protect me, if I would go: and, as the fleet was to fail the next day, I really believe I could have got fafe to Europe at that time. However, as my mafter was kind, I would not attempt to leave him; ftill remembering the old maxim, that 'honefty is the beft policy,' I fuffered them to go without me. Indeed my captain was much afraid of my leaving him and the veffel at that time, as I had fo fair an opportunity. but, I thank God, this fidelity of mine turned out much to my advantage hereafter, when I did not in the leaft think of it; and made me fo much in favour with the captain, that he ufed now and then to teach me fome parts of navigation him-

himself, but some of our passengers,.
and others, seeing this, found much
fault with him for it, saying it was a.
very dangerous thing to let a negro
know navigation; thus I was hindered
again in my pursuits. About the latter end of the year 1764, my master
bought a larger sloop, called the Pru-
dence, about seventy or eighty tons,
of which my captain had the command. I went with him into this vessel, and we took a load of new slaves
for Georgia and Charles Town. My
master now left me entirely to the
captain, though he still wished for me
to be with him; but I, who always
much wished to lose sight of the West
Indies, was not a little rejoiced at the
thoughts of seeing any other country.
Therefore, relying on the goodness of
my captain, I got ready all the little
venture I could; and, when the vessel

was

was ready, we failed to my great joy. When we got to our deftined places, Georgia and Charles Town, I expected I fhould have an opportunity of felling my little property to advantage: but here, particularly in Charles Town, I met with buyers, white men, who impofed on me as in other places. Notwithftanding, I was refolved to have fortitude, thinking no lot or trial too hard when kind Heaven is the rewarder.

We foon got loaded again, and returned to Montferrat; and there, amongft the reft of the iflands, I fold my goods well; and in this manner I continued trading during the year 1764; meeting with various fcenes of impofition, as ufual. After this, my mafter fitted out his veffel for Philadelphia, in the year 1765; and during the time we were loading her, and getting ready

ready for the voyage, I worked with
redoubled alacrity, from the hope of
getting money enough by thefe voyages
to buy my freedom, in time, if it fhould
pleafe God, and alfo to fee the town
of Philadelphia, which I had heard a
great deal about for fome years paft;
befides which, I had always longed
to prove my mafter's prom'fe the firft
day I came to him. In the midft of
thefe elevated ideas, ard while I was
about getting my little merchandize
in readinefs, one Sunday my mafter
fent for me to his houfe. When I
came there I found him and the captain together, and, on my going in, I
was ftruck with aftonifhment at his
telling me he heard that I meant to run
away from him when I got to Philadelphia 'And therefore,' faid he, 'I
' muft fell you again. you coft me a
' great deal of money, no lefs than
' forty

'forty pounds sterling, and it will
'not do to lose so much. You are a
'valuable fellow,' continued he; 'and
'I can get any day for you one hun-
'dred guineas, from many gentlemen
'in this island.' And then he told
me of Captain Doran's brother-in-law,
a severe master, who ever wanted to
buy me to make me his overseer. My
captain also said he could get much
more than a hundred guineas for me
in Carolina. This I knew to be a fact,
for the gentleman that wanted to buy
me came off several times on board of
us, and spoke to me to live with him,
and said he would use me well. When
I asked what work he would put me to,
he said, as I was a sailor, he would
make me a captain of one of his rice
vessels. But I refused: and fearing
at the same time, by a sudden turn I
saw in the captain's temper, he might
mean

mean to fell me, I told the gentleman
I would not live with him on any condition, and that I certainly would run
away with his veffel: but he faid he
did not fear that, as he would catch
him again; and then he told me how
cruelly he would ferve me if I fhould
do fo. My captain, however, gave
him to underftand that I knew fomething of navigation: fo he thought
better of it; and, to my great joy,
he went away. I now told my mafter
I did not fay I would run away in Philadelphia; neither did I mean it, as he
did not ufe me ill, nor yet the captain:
for if they did I certainly would have
made fome attempts before now; but
as I thought that if it were God's will
I ever fhould be freed it would be fo,
and, on the contrary, if it was not his
will it would not happen; fo I hoped
if ever I were freed, whilft I was ufed
well,

well, it should be by honest means; but as I could not help myself, he must do as he pleased; I could only hope and trust to the God of Heaven, and at that instant my mind was big with inventions and full of schemes to escape. I then appealed to the captain whether he ever saw any sign of my making the least attempt to run away, and asked him if I did not always come on board according to the time for which he gave me liberty, and, more particularly, when all our men left us at Gaurdeloupe and went on board of the French fleet, and advised me to go with them, whether I might not, and that he could not have got me again. To my no small surprise, and very great joy, the captain confirmed every syllable that I had said; and even more for he said he had tried different times to see if I

would

would make any attempt of this kind, both at St. Euftatia and in America, and he never found that I made the fmallest, but on the contrary, I always came on board according to his orders, and he did really believe, if I ever meant to run away, that, as I could never have had a better opportunity, I would have done it the night the mate and all the people left our veffel at Gaurdeloupe. The captain then informed my mafter, who had been thus impofed on by our mate, (though I did not know who was my enemy,) the reafon the mate had for impofing this lie upon him, which was, becaufe I had acquainted the captain of the provifions the mate had given away or taken out of the veffel. This fpeech of the captain was life to the dead to me, and inftantly my foul glorified God, and ftill more fo on hearing my mafter immediately fay that I was a fenfible fellow, and he never did intend to ufe me as a common flave; and that but for the entreaties of the captain, and his character of me, he would not have let me go from the ftores about as I had done: that alfo, in fo doing, he thought by carrying one little thing or other to different places to fell I might make money. That he alfo intended to encourage me in this, by crediting me with half a puncheon of rum and half a hogfhead of fugar at a time; fo that, from being careful, I might have money enough, in fome time, to purchafe my freedom; and, when that was the cafe, I might depend upon it he would let me have it for forty pounds fterling money, which was only the fame price he gave for me. This found gladdened my poor heart beyond meafure; though indeed

indeed it was no more than the very
idea I had formed in my mind of my
mafter long before, and I immediately
made him this reply : ' Sir, 1 always
' had that very thought of you, indeed
' I had, and that made me fo diligent
' in ferving you.' He then gave me
a large piece of filver coin, fuch as I
never had feen or had before, and told
me to get ready for the voyage, and
he would credit me with a tierce of
fugar, and another of rum ; he alfo
faid that he had two amiable fifters in
Philadelphia, fiom vhom I might get
fome neceffary things. Upon this my
noble captain defired me to go aboard ;
and, knowing the African metal, he
charged me not to fay any thing of
this matter to any body ; and he promifed that the lying mate fhould not
go with him any more. This was a
change indeed ; in the fame hour to
feel

feel the moft exquifite pain, and in
the turn of a moment the fulleft joy
It caufed in me fuch fenfations as I
was only able to exprefs in my looks,
my heart was fo overpowered with gratitude that I could have kiffed both of
their feet. When I left the room I immediately went, or rather flew, to the
veffel, which being loaded, my mafter,
as good as his word, trufted me with a
tierce of rum, and another of fugar,
when we failed, and arrived fafe at
the elegant town of Philadelphia. I
foon fold my goods here pretty well,
and in this charming place I found
every thing plentiful and cheap.

While I was in this place a very
extraordinary occurrence befell me. I
had been told one evening of a wife
woman, a Mrs. Davis, who revealed fe-
crets, foretold events, &c. I put little
faith in this ftory at faft, as I could

n u

not conceive that any mortal could
forefee the future difpofals of Providence, nor did I believe in any other
revelation than that of the Holy Scriptures ; however, I was greatly aftonifhed at feeing this woman in a dream
that night, though a perfon I never
before beheld in my life; this made
fuch an impreffion on me, that I could
not get the idea the next day out of my
mind, and I then became as anxious to
fee her as I was before indifferent; accordingly in the evening, after we left
off working, I inquired where fhe
lived, and being directed to her, to my
inexpreffible furprife, beheld the very
woman in the very fame drefs fhe appeared to me to wear in the vifion.
She immediately told me I had dreamed of her the preceding night ; related
to me many things that had happened

with a correctnefs that aftonifhed me; and finally told me I fhould not be long a flave: this was the more agreeable news, as I believed it the more readily from her having fo faithfully rel..ted the paft incidents of my life. She faid I fhould be twice in very great danger of my life within eighteen months, which, if I efcaped, I fhould afterwards go on well; fo, giving me her blefling, we parted. After ftaying here fome time till our veffel was loaded, and I had bought in my little traffic, we failed from this agreeable fpot for Montferrat, once more to encounter the raging furfs.

We arrived fafe at Montferrat, where we difcharged our cargo; and foon after that we took flaves on board for St. Euftatia, and from thence to Georgia. I had always exerted myfelf and did double work, in order to

2   make

make our voyages as short as possible; and from thus overworking myself while we were at Georgia I caught a fever and ague. I was very ill for eleven days and near dying; eternity was now exceedingly impressed on my mind, and I feared very much that awful event. I prayed the Lord therefore to spare me; and I made a promise in my mind to God, that I would be good if ever I should recover. At length, from having an eminent doctor to attend me, I was restored again to health; and soon after we got the vessel loaded, and set off for Montserrat. During the passage, as I was perfectly restored, and had much business of the vessel to mind, all my endeavours to keep up my integrity, and perform my promise to God, began to fail; and, in spite of all I could do, as we drew nearer and nearer to the

islands,

iflands, my refolutions more and more declined, as if the very air of that country or climate feemed fatal to piety. When we were fafe arrived at Montferrat, and I had got afhore, I forgot my former refolutions.—Alas! how prone is the heart to leave that God it wifhes to love! and how ftrongly do the things of this world ftrike the fenfes and captivate the foul!—After our veffel was difcharged, we foon got her ready, and took in, as ufual, fome of the poor oppreffed natives of Africa, and other negroes; we then fet off again for Georgia and Charleftown. We arrived at Georgia, and, having landed part of our cargo, proceeded to Charleftown with the remainder. While we were there I faw the town illuminated; the guns were fired, and bonfires and other demonftrations of joy fhewn, on account of the repeal of the ftamp act.

act. Here I difpofed of fome goods on my own account; the white men buying them with fmooth promifes and fair words, giving me, however, but very indifferent payment. There was one gentleman particularly who bought a puncheon of rum of me, which give me a great deal of trouble, and, although I ufed the intereft of my friendly captain, I could not obtain any thing for it; for, being a negro man, I could not oblige him to pay me. This vexed me much, not knowing how to act, and I loft fome time in feeking after this Chriftian; and though, when the Sabbath came (which the negroes ufually make their holiday) I was much inclined to go to public worfhip, I was obliged to hire fome black men to help to pull a boat acrofs the water to go in queft of this gentleman. When I found him, after much entreaty, both

N 3   from

from myfelf and my worthy captain, he at laft paid me in dollars, fome of them, however, were copper, and of confequence of no value; but he took advantage of my being a negro man, and obliged me to put up with thofe or none, although I objected to them. Immediately after, as I was trying to pafs them in the market, amongft other white men, I was abufed for of-fering to pafs bad coin; and, though I fhewed them the man I got them from, I was within one minute of being tied up and flogged without either judge or jury; however, by the help of a good pair of heels, I ran off, and fo efcaped the baftinadoes I fhould have received. I got on board as faft as I could, but ftill continued in fear of them until we failed, which I thanked God we did not long after; and I have never been amongft them fince.

We

We foon came to Georgia, where we were to complete our lading; and here worfe fate than ever attended me: for one Sunday night, as I was with fome negroes in their mafter's yard in the town of Savannah, it happened that their mafter, one Doctor Perkins, who was a very fevere and cruel man, came in drunk; and not liking to fee any ftrange negroes in his yard, he and a ruffian of a white man, he had in his fervice, befet me in an inftant, and both of them ftruck me with the firft weapons they could get hold of. I cried out as long as I could for help and mercy; but, though I gave a good account of myfelf, and he knew my captain, who lodged hard by him, it was to no purpofe. They beat and mangled me in a fhameful manner, leaving me near dead. I loft fo much blood from the wounds I received,

that

that I lay quite motionlefs, and was fo benumbed that I could not feel any thing for many hours. Early in the morning they took me away to the jail. As I did not return to the fhip all night, my captain, not knowing where I was, and being uneafy that I did not then make my appearance, he made inquiry after me; and, having found where I was, immediately came to me. As foon as the good man faw me fo cut and mangled, he could not forbear weeping, he foon got me out of jail to his lodgings, and immediately fent for the beft doctors in the place, who at firft declared it as their opinion that I could not recover. My captain on this went to all the lawyers in the town for their advice, but they told him they could do nothing for me as I was a negro. He then went to Doctor Perkins, the hero who had vanquifhed

quifhed me, and menaced him, fwearing he would be revenged of him,
and challenged him to fight.—But
cowardice is ever the companion of
cruelty—and the Doctor refufed. However, by the fkilfulnefs of one Doctor
Brady of that place, I began at laft to
amend, but, although I was fo fore and
bad with the wounds I had all over me
that I could not reft in any pofture,
yet I was in more pain on account of
the captain's uneafinefs about me than
I otherwife fhould have been. The
worthy man nurfed and watched me
all the hours of the night; and I was,
through his attention and that of the
doctor, able to get out of bed in about
fixteen or eighteen days. All this
time I was very much wanted on
board, as I ufed frequently to go up
and down the river for rafts, and other
parts of our cargo, and ftow them,

when

when the mate was fick or abfent. In
about four weeks I was able to go on
duty ; and in a fortnight after, having
got in all our lading, our veffel fet fail
for Montferrat ; and in lefs than three
weeks we arrived there fafe towards
the end of the year. This ended my
adventures in 1764; for I did not leave
Montferrat again till the beginning of
the following year.

END OF THE FIRST VOLUME.